Living a
Conscious Life

Living a Conscious Life

How to Find Peace, Wholeness, and Freedom in a Chaotic World

Donald E. Johnson

SelectBooks, Inc.
New York

This edition published by SelectBooks, Inc.
For information address SelectBooks, Inc., New York, New York.

First Edition

ISBN 978-1-59079-562-0

Cataloging-in-Publication Data

Names: Johnson, Donald E. (Executive coach), author.
Title: Living a conscious life : a thinking person's guide to peace,
   wholeness, and freedom / Donald E. Johnson.
Description: First edition. | New York : SelectBooks, [2024] | Includes
   bibliographical references and index. | Summary: "Fifty-one brief
   articles written by Don Johnson, a former monk who lived in an ashram
   for ten years before becoming a corporate consultant and executive
   coach, relay his experiences and teachings. Topics include the quest
   for inner knowledge, practicing meditation and raja yoga, changing our
   mindsets, forming happy relationships, recovering from failures, and
   finding love and peace"-- Provided by publisher.
Identifiers: LCCN 2023037115 (print) | LCCN 2023037116 (ebook) | ISBN
   9781590795620 (paperback) | ISBN 9781590795637 (ebook)
Subjects: LCSH: Self-actualization (Psychology) | Interpersonal relations.
   | Spirituality--Psychology.
Classification: LCC BF637.S4 J636 2024 (print) | LCC BF637.S4 (ebook) |
   DDC 158.1--dc23/eng/20231030
LC record available at https://lccn.loc.gov/2023037115
LC ebook record available at https://lccn.loc.gov/2023037116

Book design by Janice Benight

Manufactured in the United States of America
10 9 8 7 6 5 4 3 2 1

To all those carrying the Light
and having the courage to speak the Truth

Contents

Part Three
Building Meaningful Relationships   91

Part Four
Living a More Fulfilling Life   149

Contents   ix

Preface

Winters in Scotland are often windy and damp and especially dark. Around the end of February sunset finally starts to push past 5:30 in the evening, and shoots of tulips, bluebells, and snowdrops somehow emerge from the cold ground, signaling it's time for brighter days.

The spring of 2020 brought us glorious weather, and it also ushered in the beginning of the global pandemic. That's when this book began.

Many businesses throughout the world were hit hard by the pandemic, and my leadership consulting business was no exception. Suddenly I had plenty of time on my hands and could sit in the back garden for hours reading and playing guitar. But when I realized Medium.com, an emerging international online writing platform, had an audience thirsty for inspiration, my reading turned into writing. I thought, "I've been meditating for 48 years. I think I've got something to say."

Fortunately one of the prominent publications on Medium picked up my first few articles on meditation and communication skills, and the reader response was very positive. The more I wrote, the more I discovered that my life story and what I've learned were of interest to many people.

So for the next 18 months, that's what I tried to do—dig deep inside, write truthfully, and offer practical content. I've used my own experiences of success, failure, guilt, shame, and redemption to underscore the challenges we face in our journey to become more conscious human beings.

I hope you find my advice informative and some of my stories amusing. And more importantly, I'd be honored if the stories inspire you to continue exploring your inner world and help make the world a better place.

Acknowledgments

Thank you Kathy Sparrow, Randy Peyser, Diane Eaton, Stephanie Georgopulos, Michael Thompson, Eric Sangerma, Christine Bradstreet, Stella Vark, Nancy, Kenzi and Kenichi at SelectBooks and all the people who reviewed the first draft of this book and gave me your support.

Photos of the author by Patricia Ramaer

Introduction

In July 1972, I had a life-changing spiritual awakening. I was 20 years old. While working at a summer job at Ohio Wesleyan University, I met a young woman who told me about a young Indian guru named Maharaji who could reveal an inner knowledge of peace.

I woke up later that night after having a vivid dream, and a powerful, eerie sense of déjà vu swept over me. A profound sense of peace washed through me. My breath quickened, my eyes filled with tears, and I began to sob uncontrollably. I felt like the door to my soul had cracked open.

I knew I had to learn more, and within a few months I found myself sitting in a small room with a dozen other people learning ancient techniques of raja yoga taught by one of Maharaji's close followers. My journey to discover the inner world of the soul was underway.

I spent the next ten years living in ashrams (which means "shelter" in Hindi) throughout the world, having taken vows of poverty, chastity, and obedience.

When I was in my early 30s, the ashrams closed. It seemed a good time to work toward a career in the leadership development industry. But first, I paid my dues doing menial jobs. After a year of getting rejected by dozens of corporate training jobs, I got a lucky break and received an offer to teach sales at a bank in Philadelphia.

A few years later, I took a job at Zenger Miller, a premier leadership development firm in the '80s and '90s founded and led by Jack Zenger, a brilliant thought leader and businessman. For the next 16 years, I received a significant education in leadership, communication, and team principles and skills while having jobs in consulting, sales, and teaching leadership.

I left in 2004, and a few years later joined Axialent, a boutique culture transformation company founded by Fred Kofman, author of *Conscious Business.* He and his partner thought I could bring something unique to their company based on my corporate training experience.

That turned out not to be the case. However, they did need executive coaches and facilitators since the business was growing exponentially. So, for the next four years I learned from some of the sharpest minds in the industry while providing coaching and leadership development to some of the most well-known brands in the world, including Google, Microsoft, YouTube, and Yahoo!. It was profoundly satisfying work.

My time at Axialent reignited my spiritual practices—company meetings began with meditation and self-reflection. The culture encouraged authenticity, truth-telling, honoring your word, and doing "inner work" for self-improvement. I studied the influence of mindsets, attitudes, and beliefs about human behavior and read the work of Ken Wilber, Don Beck, Fernando Flores, Victor Frankl, Peter Senge, Jim Collins, and many other great thinkers.

When I left Axialent, I joined Insights Learning & Development, a Scottish firm that created a Jungian-based personality profile used to build more self-awareness. I reunited with Connie Bentley, someone I'd worked with at Zenger Miller, and, with the help of a great team of people, we almost tripled the size of the U.S. business in five years.

In the fall of 2016, after my second marriage unwound, I fell in love with a Scottish woman and a year later closed the door on my full-time corporate career. I was proud of what I had achieved but was burnt out. I spent months in Scotland with her, recovering, healing, and trying to figure out what I wanted to do with the rest of my life.

We made plans to get married, and in 2019, I moved to Scotland. I launched a consulting business offering leadership, executive coaching, and personality assessments. Without knowing it, I planted the seeds of writing a book by beginning to journal again.

These seeds grew during the pandemic, manifesting in dozens of articles that reflected my experiences as a monk and meditator, a parent, a husband, and a consultant. After several years of rewriting and editing, my first book was born.

PART 1

For the Heart

When You Live from Your Heart, No One Forgets What You Leave Behind

How a very cool guy changed my life forever

"Erection."

"Louder, please."

"Erection!"

My tenth-grade English teacher, Joel Kabatznick, was doing his "Words of the Week Club" routine. Every Friday, he'd spend about ten minutes teaching us words we didn't know, like "idiosyncrasy" or "meretricious." And every so often, he'd slip in his brand of sex education. The class would squirm and blush when he had us say things every teenager thought about but would never say in public.

Mr. Kabatznick was by far the most memorable, inspiring, and hippest teacher I ever had. With his bushy hair and thick-rimmed glasses, white shirt, crazy tie, and crumpled dark suit hanging loosely on his muscled, five-foot-eight-inch frame, he was an eclectic-looking and oddly behaving man. His teaching methods were no less idiosyncratic. While talking about the symbolism of Captain Ahab riding Moby Dick, he'd grab a piece of chalk and start writing on the chalkboard, his jacket brushing up against the board gathering white dust. He'd continue writing to the end of the chalkboard, and then onto the wall, then the door. It was as if he had lost track of time and space. Then he'd whirl around and face the class, his clothes covered in dust, and grin as if he'd just come back into his body. We'd watch him in amazement. No other teacher was putting on this kind of show. We were all in.

He knew how to entertain and engage resistant, bored, apathetic students. To a 15-year-old, he appeared to be like a parent because he was an authority figure, but he didn't behave like a parent. He created an atmosphere in which I learned to love modern literature as we read and discussed *The Catcher in the Rye*, *A Separate Peace*, *To Kill a Mockingbird*, and many other great American novels.

He was funny and passionate and ran a tight ship. Nobody mouthed off and got away with it, and no one was humiliated. It was apparent he loved what he did. Somehow that stuck with me as a kid—seeing an adult who loved his work and lived from his heart. I walked away from his class wanting to find something I loved to do, too.

When I found my way into corporate sales training, I remember asking myself, *How can I be like Kabatznick? How can I engage people as he did? How can my sessions be interesting, engaging, and impactful?*

Well, I did the best I could, but I was no Joel Kabatznick. It wasn't until later in my career that I understood his secret. He understood what many others fail to recognize: *his job was not to teach; it was to help people learn.* I think he was successful because he understood the difference.

I thought about him recently and did a quick Google search. Teaching almost to his last breath, he died at the age of 54 in 1995 in Alaska from multiple sclerosis complications. The postings I read from students he taught around the world reflected my memories of him. He was a kind, brilliant man who connected to and helped anyone lucky enough to know him. His sister wrote this remembrance:

> His students remember him for his eccentric behavior, bizarre taste in clothes, genuine interest in them, and unique teaching style. Joel knew the importance of laughter and utilized it in his classes, often at his own expense.
>
> He always advocated on his student's behalf and related to them as his friends. One of Joel's greatest gifts to them was his belief in praise rather than criticism. Three of his favorite words were "You are good."

I thought about the power of those words. "You are good." So simple, really. How many of us who have self-doubt, and perhaps had failures in our personal life or business, longed to hear those words when we were down? Many of us live our lives comparing our lives to others. We judge our successes by what others are doing or worry we are missing out because we haven't "found" ourselves—our calling, the perfect job, or the ideal lover. We make ourselves nuts when we see a colleague do something brilliant, and while acknowledging it publicly, we privately skewer ourselves for not having done it first. How often do we stop this berating and tell ourselves, "You are good"? Probably not enough.

Joel struggled with multiple sclerosis throughout his adult life; he'd walked with a cane since he was 28. He shrugged his health issues off as "old football injuries" and proved they didn't keep him from living life on his own terms or from being a man who brought joy to the people around him. They didn't stop him from being someone who celebrated the importance of laughter, made learning fun, supported his students without criticism, related to them as friends, and counseled those who got into trouble. What a beautiful man.

*　*　*

I like to imagine he's still around in his crumpled dark suit, a piece of chalk in his hand, smiling and saying, "Remember: you are good."

When you live from your heart, no one forgets what you leave behind.

A Failed Vasectomy Changed My Life

Sometimes the Universe has other plans

I was nervous when I walked through the door of the clinic. I was even more nervous as I lay on the table in my surgical gown, legs apart, the nurse happily shaving me.

Maybe they gave me some Valium. I really can't remember, but I doubt it. I do remember when the doc brought out the needle filled with local anesthesia. It was the largest I'd ever seen, and it would be inserted not once but twice into my now clean-shaven . . . yes—those.

"You're going to feel a little pinch now." Ouch. Thanks for that.

Out came the snips, knives, surgical saws, and whatever else was needed to cut the *vas deferens*, the tubes that carry the sperm to the launch pad. I didn't pass out, perhaps because the doc and the nurse talked about their weekend plans and how the local football team was doing during the entire pre-op phase. Did they realize I was lying there on the table, scared out of my mind? I figured they didn't attend the class on helping patients feel like they care about them. The docs just continued their banter as they sliced and diced. Then, all of a sudden, it was over.

"Just put some ice on it and rest. You might get some swelling for a few days, but don't worry about it. You'll be fine."

The whole thing wasn't humorous at all. What was rather funny, if you want to call it that, was bringing in a sample a month later to check for live bullets.

"Well, Mr. Johnson—heh heh—please be advised that you should not have unprotected sex yet. You've still got live sperm in your semen. This is quite normal. Please bring another sample in six weeks."

Great. I'll do that. More samples. Same results. I repeated this for the next nine months.

A few years earlier

Before all the snipping, my wife Polly became pregnant, and I was feeling overwhelmed. We were living hand-to-mouth, and my employer—a bank—would soon go bust. The baby was unplanned, and as much as I wanted children, the timing was a few years ahead of my master plan. Nine months later, my daughter was born. I cut the cord and welcomed her into the world with loving arms, but I still felt overcome by the responsibility of raising a kid.

And Polly wanted another child soon. I certainly did not. We found some therapists, a husband and wife team, and got to work. After a few joint sessions, we split off into individual sessions. My therapist started to unpack my cluttered psyche:

"How is your relationship with your father?"

"Terrible," I replied.

"Okay. Let's start there."

We talked, he got in my face, and I cried. I punched the leather pillows on his couch and screamed at the top of my lungs.

I journaled about my father and then wrote letters to him. He and I started communicating again—a little.

Meanwhile, I'm bringing in semen samples loaded up with live sperm. After nine months, I brought in one last sample. It tested positive. The failure rate of vasectomies is .2 %, which means that one or two out of 1,000 procedures are unsuccessful. For those guys, the vas deferens grow back together. Or, in my case, maybe my very attentive medical team never cut them at all.

Awakening

After that last positive sample, I realized I've been working my ass off with my shrink to make peace with my father and to prepare to . . . what . . . *have another kid? Hmm.* Maybe, I still hadn't decided yet.

I had concluded one thing. My father wasn't as bad as I thought. He may have been an aggressive, over-controlling, womanizing,

perfectionistic racist. but he was also a charming, patriotic, successful, intelligent man doing the best he could with the tools he had.
And he was my father.

So, I opened the door to forgiveness and the possibility of recon-
ciliation. I had learned a lot from him and figured I could keep the
good stuff—the value of hard work, storytelling, humor, persistence,
and problem-solving—and eliminate the bad stuff. I began to feel a
bit more prepared to be a better parent. And guess what? After the
failed vasectomy, I wanted to have another kid.

The Universe is at work

When my son was born nine months later, I was thrilled. Everything made more sense now: The bad feeling about the doc from the
beginning; the vasectomy that never worked; the therapy to get my
head straight and rid myself of my fatherly rage; the time I needed
to decide on wanting a second child. I thought, *"Damn. If the Universe
wants something to happen, it will. If it doesn't, it won't."* For whatever
reason, I was given a chance to be a father to my son—and hopefully, a good one.

Call it what you want. Coincidence. Serendipity. Good luck. Bad
luck. Destiny. For me, it was a startling reminder that while I might
want to take control of my life—and my sperm, damn it—I don't call
all the shots. The Universe does. And it's looking out for me, probably more than I'll ever know. I've got to do my part, trust the Higher
Power, and fully accept what happens.

The Australian novelist Morris West describes the nature of life
beautifully in *The Shoes of the Fisherman*:

> It costs so much to be a full human being that there are very
> few who have the enlightenment, or the courage to pay the
> price . . . One has to abandon altogether the search for secu-
> rity and reach out to the risk of living with both arms. One has
> to embrace life like a lover, and yet demand no easy return of

love. One has to accept pain as a condition of existence. One has to court doubt and darkness as the cost of knowing. One needs a will stubborn in conflict, but apt always to the total acceptance of every consequence of living and dying.

I vowed I would never treat my son like I was treated when I was growing up. We always stayed on the same side of the fence. I didn't tell my son to cut his hair, how to dress, or what music to listen to. Nor did I encourage him to fight in a war we shouldn't be in or ridicule his personal choices. However, I'm sure I did damage somewhere, and if he does go to therapy, he and his shrink will have plenty of work to do.

Shortly after his birth, I got another vasectomy. Different doc. This guy said, "Don't worry, pal, I'm going to fix you for good." It worked this time. Thank f*@k.

*   *   *

Sometimes we think we know what we want. Sometimes the Universe has other plans.

The Power of
Healing Broken Relationships

When you forgive, you grow

My father was a high-achieving, sharp-looking, charismatic, entertaining guy. He provided for our family, and I learned a lot from him. He taught me the importance of hard work, paying attention to details, asking for what you want, anticipating what can happen, being a good conversationalist, and being friendly to and respectful of others.

He could also be a short-tempered, controlling, overbearing, critical, and perfectionist pain in the ass. As with anyone, overused strengths can become weaknesses. Worse, I heard many racist and misogynist remarks from him throughout my life. He was far from perfect, but he was my father.

After the Korean War he left the military and applied for a sales job at a pharmaceutical company in New York, saying he would work for no pay until he proved himself. They took him, and he went on to have a highly successful, 30-year sales career, eventually retiring from an executive position.

Growing up

Between his job responsibilities and his love for golf, my father wasn't around much when I was growing up. If I went to the golf course with him, things usually ended up with my melting down as he tried to over-instruct me. Eventually, the sport made me miserable, and I quit playing. By the time I got to high school, my father and I were miles apart. I didn't understand him, and he didn't understand me.

I went off to college, grew my hair long, and went full counterculture. I protested the Vietnam War, became a conscientious objector, took drugs, studied just enough to get by, and graduated near the bottom of my class. I collected my English literature degree pleasantly stoned. A few months later, I dropped out of mainstream society, moved into an ashram, and followed an Indian guru for the next ten years.

My path was not what my father had in mind. He'd just paid a small fortune for my education, and now I was practicing meditation and living like a monk in some run-down hippie house in Boston. As he teed off at his swanky country club, what could he say to his friends whose sons were promising young attorneys or med students? "Oh yeah, my kid is a monk worshipping a teenaged Indian boy"? Much later, I realized how he suffered, but I didn't care back then. I wasn't interested in conforming to his idea of the "perfect son." I needed to find my own way.

On my infrequent visits home, sitting at the family dinner table with my mother and sisters, my father ridiculed me about the "guru." I wanted to punch him in the face, but I just looked at him and let it go, feeling embarrassed for him. He was arrogant and closed-minded, and I knew nothing I could say would change his mind.

My father and I didn't talk much during the ten years I was a monk. But when I was 33, things took a turn for the better. I left the ashram, got married, and started working in corporate America. I was now in "his world," and we could talk about marriage, business, homeownership, and sports.

Facing the past

My daughter was born when I was 37, and I began to feel the raw responsibility of raising a family. When I became a monk at 23, I grew spiritually, but I didn't grow psychologically. All my suppressed, critical, and short-tempered bullshit started to surface. I felt like I was becoming my father. I knew one thing: I didn't want to treat my children the way my father treated me.

I found a good shrink, a guy named John. John told me I had to deal with my wounds, particularly the one with my father. I was angry because I never had a father who understood me. I was pissed off by his absence in my life, the way he opposed my choices, and how he ridiculed me for ten years. To get the anger out of my body, John had me pounding leather pillows and screaming at the top of my lungs. I cried my eyes out. He suggested I write a letter to my father, telling him what it was like to grow up with him and what I wanted now. Initially, I struggled. I left those sessions exhausted, but I knew something good was happening.

I'd write a letter to my father, show John a draft of it, and he'd say it wasn't good enough. Soon, I'd show him another. After many rounds of these exchanges, I finally got one in acceptable condition, and off it went.

Steps to resolution

The letter my father wrote in response kick-started my healing process:

> You remember clashing on a number of issues when you were young, afraid of me, my anger, and pickiness. I must say that I recall some of those moments, and it saddens me to think of them now. I regret them with all my heart and know my fuse was too short. I had a lot of insecurities and only wanted you to be the best. You were and are such a great son. I have always loved you and again regret my inability to convey that message properly.

My father had never said anything like that to me before. I wrote him back a long letter, thanking him and letting him know how much his words meant. Over the next ten years, my father and I were pleasant to each other, but we never talked about those letters or our relationship. When I turned 55, I realized his son had become a man; I wanted to have a face-to-face conversation with him before he passed away. He was 81, and his health was beginning to decline. During my next visit, I asked him if we could talk, and he consented.

I told him what it was like growing up under his heavy hand and how I needed to break free. I explained why I joined a spiritual movement and lived like a monk for ten years. I told him that I wanted his love and support, not his opposition.

He listened quietly and apologized for the difficulties he caused in our relationship. Then he told me his side of the story. I learned that for those ten years, my father was worried about me constantly. He didn't know where I was or what I was doing, and he didn't know how to connect with me. Tears welled up in my eyes as I listened to him. I could feel the heaviness and the loneliness of his heart all those years he felt he didn't have a son.

Forgiveness

Coincidentally, my son was a young teenager at the time, and my worst nightmare would have been losing connection with him or having him walk away from me. Until my conversation with my father, I had never understood how things looked through his eyes. And there, sitting across from me, was my dad, telling me this happened to him. Tears streamed down his face, too. Later that evening, I crawled into bed and cried uncontrollably.

I finally understood that my father had done the best he could with what he had. If I hadn't fully forgiven him before, I certainly did then. I was at peace; I'd done all that I could. He lived another ten years and then passed away in his sleep in 2016 at the age of 91.

Like all of us, my father was flawed and fabulous. Accepting him as he was, however long that took, helped me accept myself more fully. I gradually eased up on my perfectionism. I became more forgiving and tolerant of my mistakes and more effective at managing my negative self-talk. I was able to take constructive criticism with less self-flagellation. Over time, I became more forgiving and patient with others, too.

As my kids grew into their 20s, I'd occasionally catch myself before saying something I shouldn't. Still, there were times when the offending words just leaked out. But no matter what was said that I regretted, I made sure my kids were loved and supported. I wasn't a perfect parent by any means, but I worked hard to make sure they knew I was there for them and we could always resolve disagreements.

I recently started playing golf again. I'm really enjoying it, and as I walk down the fairways I remember my dad. I think he'd be pleased I'm finally playing the game he loved so much.

*   *   *

Despite my progress, my work never ends. A few years ago, my kids gave me a hoodie for Christmas with the words "In Control" printed on the front.

"Really? Still?" I asked them.

They spoke with big smiles. "Yes, Dad. Sometimes you still are a control freak."

"I'm trying. I really am."

They laughed. "Yeah, you've definitely gotten better."

Hearing that was a relief.

How to Light Up a Room Without Stepping Inside

Kindness is a knock on the door

Friday night. The candles flickered on the dining room table. The just-out-of-the-oven homemade pizza lay on the wooden cutting boards, ready to slice. My wife, Mariclaire, picked up her glass of red wine. I did the same, and we toasted our good fortune—a roof over our heads, good food, our health, and happiness.

I heard a knock on the front door.

"Must be another Amazon delivery. I probably ordered something. They'll leave it there," I said.

But Mariclaire insisted. "I don't know. Let me go check."

I heard some voices, and, a minute later, she came back inside. "That was the guy we saw on the street a few weeks ago," she said. "The trunk of your car was wide open, and he wanted us to know."

"Really? Wow, that's nice of him."

When we receive kindness, we're reminded of the goodness in human beings, and that can shift our focus from what's wrong in the world to what is right. When we see kindness in others, we recognize it in ourselves and discover we want to be a person who is kind. We intuitively know kindness is our true nature.

We're living in a time of historic transformation right now. An uncertain future can trigger self-protective, defensive, and "let me take care of me" behaviors. It's understandable. Minor annoyances might get under your skin more easily. What used to slide right off your back now makes you short with people. There have been days when I've become the irritable version of myself. It's not real pleasant—but maybe it's not the uncertainty; perhaps it's just the grind of everyday life.

You might be tired, busy, and distracted. It might be easy to drift off and forget to ask your partner if they want a refill for their coffee when you go get yours. Instead of offering to cook dinner, you hesitate because you don't want to take on any more. But you think about it later and wonder if you're becoming small-minded.

If any of this sounds like you, the bad news is you've momentarily become disconnected from the real you. The good news is your true self is full of kindness, and you can quickly reconnect. It's been said there are two kinds of people in the world—those who light up a room when they enter and those who light it up when they leave. Kind people light up a room; they shine from the inside.

Shine from the inside: five easy practices

Here are five easy practices to help you shine from the inside—and light up a room.

1. Be grateful

Keith J. Cunningham, the best-selling author of, *The Road Less Stupid: Advice from the Chairman of the Board*, writes: "Happiness is only available through gratitude. It's gratitude that forces you to focus on the present rather than on regrets about the past and fears of the future. Fulfillment is only available by giving what you've got. The triumph of happiness and fulfillment is found through gratitude and contribution."

Most nights, before we go to sleep, Mariclaire and I hold hands and say what we feel grateful for. Other people I know journal in the morning, reminding themselves what they are thankful for. It doesn't matter if you're grateful for big things—like getting a new job or a promotion—or if you're thankful for everyday things like seeing the sunrise or drinking a good cup of coffee. Appreciating what we have ignites positive energy in the body and mind. It opens our hearts, keeps us humble, and reminds us of our good fortune. When we're grateful, we are more resilient, more joyful, and more radiant. Make gratitude a daily practice.

2. Recharge

Burnout is real. Our bodies and minds need time to heal when we work hard. Being brain dead isn't just a metaphor. When I finish a week of writing, my brain feels soft and my thinking is dull. My brain needs time to heal and recharge, time to unplug and detox. What works for me is moving my body, getting fresh air, and staying off my devices. Doing something as simple as taking ten deep breaths will restore needed oxygen to the brain. Better yet, carve out "you" time each day—at least ten minutes when you do nothing but sit quietly and meditate or breathe or think.

When we go within like this, we take care of our inner self and connect with the source of joy, inspiration, and happiness. When we feel restored, we can take care of others. When they interact with us, they see hope, and they feel our joy. When we're alive and lit up, we can light others up.

3. Keep your mind clean

Stories of suffering, chaos, greed, and misinformation in the mainstream media outweigh messages of hope. Our minds and bodies are like sponges; we absorb that negative energy. So, we need to keep our psyches clean to be the best version of ourselves. I recommend that you limit or eliminate any dependency on watching mainstream news. If you do watch it, balance it with at least as much time viewing or hearing positive messaging. Hang out with optimistic people. Don't get involved in blaming and complaining.

Before I go to sleep, I either pray, read positive affirmations, or ask the Universe for guidance. Over time, I've found it clears any negative messaging leftover from the day while building new, resilient thought patterns. Keep your energy up.

4. Find joy in the little things

For many centuries, indigenous people, tribes, and clans did not stop singing, dancing, and finding joy in whatever they had even when they were suffering. They sustained themselves by bringing their hearts into everyday life, no matter how difficult it was. Bring joy into *your* life each day by doing things that make you happy. Think of these as little moments of luxury that are just for you. You might choose to take a walk or run a warm bath with candles, have a piece of rich dark chocolate, cook a favorite food, watch a great TV show, sing if you like singing or dance if you want to dance. Treat yourself with kindness; it will help stimulate joy.

5. Use your words wisely

Our words create our world. A slight shift in the way we speak can help us maintain openness and kindness and avoid unnecessary friction. Here are some examples:

> Instead of saying, "You're not making any sense,"
> say, "I'm having trouble understanding you."

> Instead of saying, "You always interrupt me,"
> say, "Please let me finish."

> Instead of saying, "You handled the situation quite well, but you missed something,"
> say, "You handled the situation quite well, and I noticed (x). What do you think about that?"

> Instead of saying, "Are you still working on your pet project?"
> say, "How is the project coming along?"

> Instead of saying, "You've got it all wrong,"
> say, "I have a concern about what you are working on. Can we discuss it?"

> Speak with respect and kindness.

* * *

I went out and closed the trunk of my car, thinking about how this guy's small act of kindness affected me. I thought about the type of person he is—generous, thoughtful, and honest. He inspired me, reminding me I have those qualities too.

I looked up at the full moon low in the February sky. It was beaming like a giant celestial spotlight, the last one of the winter. I thought, *"Damn. Can't we all be kinder to ourselves and each other and make the world a better place to live?"* Sure we can. All it takes is a pleasant word to a stranger, an offer of help to a friend in a jam, a random thank-you card to your partner, or an act of giving someone your uninterrupted attention while they speak with you.

I came back inside, sat down, sliced up the pizza, and thanked Mariclaire for answering the door. She looked at me. "That guy didn't even have to walk in the room to light it up," she said. "He just knocked."

The Path to Finding Love Can Be a Long and Winding Road

Keep a candle in your window

T wenty years ago, I stepped into an elevator in a Vancouver hotel for a company meeting. A woman stood waiting inside, and our eyes met instantly. She was adorable—short blond hair, blue eyes, and a friendly smile. Someone introduced us, and later we had our first conversation at a group dinner. Over the next few days, we spoke some more.

We flew home on the same flight to Philadelphia and flirted shamelessly as we picked up our baggage. I called her a few days later, and she agreed to meet for dinner—the quiet fires of attraction smoldering. We fanned the flames again a few nights after that at a small neighborhood restaurant near her home.

Our arms slid around each other as I ordered drinks at the bar, waiting for a table. Her perfume washed over me as we leaned into each other. A raw desire to merge with her burned through every cell of my body; it was unlike anything I'd ever experienced. We ate—or tried to eat—but the adrenalin squashed most of the hunger. There was no reason to linger, so we drove the winding road on the banks of the Schuykill River back to her place. Like a teenager about to lose his virginity—I was excited, nervous, and not quite ready. We both knew what was about to happen.

The next day, we were in the office, business as usual, except I was completely stoned on every love chemical known to man coursing through my body. Lit up like torches, we fell more deeply in love as we worked together for the next six months. I was hooked, and her love drugs were good, deeply satisfying, and wickedly addicting.

Work took us to a number of cities, and we made adventures out of them. Dinners out. Live music. Broadway shows. Eating by candle-light. Running back to the hotel in the warm summer rain, splashing through puddles, getting drenched, and laughing like kids. Spending time wrapped in each other's arms.

It was a perfect romance except for one thing. Each of us was married to someone else.

After six months, her husband returned from an overseas assign-ment and found evidence of our relationship on her computer. My wife uncovered the truth, too. It became a giant, ugly train wreck. I was embarrassed and ashamed of my behavior, as was she.

We met as lovers for one final time, walking down to the river to say our goodbyes. I imagined dark angels watching over us as we cried and cried and cried some more. We knew all along we were way out of bounds, both of us swept away, caught up in recklessness, and now it was over.

A few days later, we were back at work. It was surreal to just be friends again. Making things even more emotionally challenging, we traveled together for the next four months on business—overnights in hotels, separate rooms, one thin wall between us. Half hoping for the knock on my door that never came, sleep was intermittent and lonely.

Soon after that, she left the company to start her own business. We continued to see each other for lunch occasionally until she decided she wanted to cut off all communication between us and focus on her marriage. I understood it intellectually, but I was still in love, hurt, and angry. I wrote her a nasty note. She showed up in my dreams; It was hard for me to forget her. I began to express my love and angst through writing and recording half a dozen songs—they were some of the best songs I'd ever composed. She was my muse.

A few years went by. Her marriage remained intact as her husband gradually and graciously forgave her. My wife, although deeply wounded, did everything she could to heal her heart and forgive me. We tried hard to make it work, but my heartbreak haunted me. I couldn't find my way back into the marriage.

Three years later, after 17 years of marriage, we split amicably, but not without a great deal of suffering. Fortunately, we've remained good friends, for which I'm deeply grateful.

A few years after the divorce, I flew home from a business trip and walked through the terminal toward the parking garage. The elevator was in front of me, the doors just about to close. I hurried ever so slightly and slipped in as the doors closed.

A woman was in the elevator, her back to me. She turned around, and it was her—my muse. We were stunned; the icy goodbye from the past melted in a long, warm hug. I whispered an apology for the note I had written her. She said, "Don't worry about it." We got out of the elevator and talked for a while, agreeing to have lunch soon.

The lunch and the conversation were lovely, and so was the gentle kiss as we said goodbye, but it wasn't the same. She'd changed, and so had I. The heat of the romance was long gone, but the friendship was strong. Like any relationship, it had evolved. We asked each other what it all meant—another perfectly orchestrated meeting in an elevator within an enormous city airport. Perhaps it meant nothing, or maybe it was so I could finally heal and know her as a friend—in the light—without slipping through the shadows of an illicit affair?

And I did heal. We stayed in touch over the next ten years through phone calls and occasional meetings. We discovered we sincerely cared for each other, and as a result, we're still friends to this day— her husband is well aware of our friendship.

As I mentioned earlier, I remarried. But before I moved to Scotland, Mariclaire and I took a walk in a large park and planned to go to lunch. As we walked, we passed a woman wearing sunglasses and a baseball hat sitting on a bench. I glanced at her.

"Kind of looks like her," I thought.

When we got to the restaurant, I said to Mariclaire, "That might have been the woman I've told you about. I'd like to go over to her to say "hello." Are you okay with that?"

"Yes. You should," she said.

I walked outside. I was right. It was her. I thought, *"This is crazy. Is there no end to how we keep showing up in each other's lives?"*

She smiled, stood up, and hugged me.

"I'm finally happy," I told her. "And I'd like you to meet my wife."

She agreed and walked into the restaurant with me. I watched as the two women, each with a unique place in my life, came together, hugging each other as if they'd been friends for years.

When she left a few minutes later, Mariclaire said she knew we would meet her that day.

I smiled and laughed, marveling at the elegance and serendipity of it all. The seemingly disparate, unexplainable, you-can't-make-it-up moments in life, when strung together, help make a bit more sense out of the mysteries of life and the journey to resolution and love.

* * *

Never give up on your dreams. You may make seemingly wrong turns, but keep your faith and trust in the Universe. You never know what can happen.

You're the Only Person Who Needs to Know How Good You Are

Self-doubt is not your friend

I don't know about you, but sometimes I doubt myself. I doubt I can write another decent article; I doubt an email I sent to someone will be well-received; I doubt I can improve my golf game; I doubt I'm a good enough parent. I remember sending an email to a coaching client, who works in a very high-pressured, toxic environment, challenging him not to forget that the essence of leadership is about spirit. I thought that was innocent enough. But after I sent it, I began to wonder how he would react to it. I didn't hear from him for a few days, so a bit of doubt appeared. Maybe it was the wrong thing at the wrong time? Perhaps he's too worn out even to consider it?

Then I got this response from him:

> *Hi Don,*
>
> *Your timing is perfect. I feel like lumps are being taken out of me, and suddenly, I am becoming very stretched. We both know the toxic environment will not allow any breathing space, so I must find my own soul, as you say.*

What am I worrying about? Doubt is paralyzing. It is vaporous, invisible matter filling the space that can only exist in the absence of wholeness—the absence of our being present, of being in touch with our real selves. It eats away at our self-confidence, and before we know it, we're looking for external validation because we've become separated from ourselves, our goodness, and who we are.

When doubt floats in, insecurity takes over.

Insecurity is forgetting we are good the way we are. We compensate by getting involved, trying to fit in, or trying to please others so we can feel accepted and validated. Sure, it's important that we have a positive reputation in the world. But you don't build a strong sense of self by worrying about how others perceive you and if you're good enough for them. There's only one person who needs to know how good you are—*you.*

I learned a great lesson about this many years ago. As a young kid, I dreamed of playing professional basketball. For years, I practiced every day for hours and hours. I was very average, but I had a dream to play in front of a big crowd and hear them roar for the home team, just like the pros did.

One day, I had my chance. A heavy winter storm blew into suburban Boston on a weekday morning in December. When I got to school, the storm picked up even more. Many businesses closed early, but the last high school basketball game of the season was on. My team was playing our archrival, the best in the league. Before the game, the locker room was unusually quiet—many of our top players never even got to school that day. After we got dressed, the coach looked at me and said, "You're starting today, and you're going to guard the other team's top scorer.

You're quick, and I want you to stay with him—everywhere. Defense, Johnson. That's what I want you to do." I was not one of the top players, rarely got in any of the games, and spent the entire season sitting on the bench, so this was a big deal for me. When you never play, you're never really sure if you can perform in prime time.

We walked into the gym. Typically, the stands were full. However, that day, the place was empty. The game started, and I scored the first basket. We pulled ahead as the game went on. The team played well. I did my job guarding my opponent, and we won the game by six points, a big upset for us.

I scored seven points. Not much, I know, but it was the most I ever scored in a game. I was stunned and happy we won, but no one saw it happen—no family or friends, no media, and nobody was cheering.

It was the last high school basketball game I ever played. Still, I knew I played well, and I discovered I was better than I thought.

Self-doubt? Gone. I knew I could play under the lights. Don't doubt yourself. You're good the way you are, and you're the only person who needs to know it.

Tenacity Pays Off

I wanna thank me for believing in me

At 32 years of age I was penniless. I had nothing, not a dime. No cash, no savings, no car, no nothing. I got on my feet thanks to a guy named Henry Reif, who took a chance and loaned me a few thousand bucks. Thank you again, Henry.

It's easy to forget where we came from and what we did along the way. And there are times when it's good to remember your roots and recognize the most important factor in your success—*you*.

Don't get me wrong, I'm a big believer in gratitude, thanking the Henry Reifs of the world and the serendipity of the Universe, but I also believe it's what we do with what we are given that counts.

What I do matters. What you do matters.

None of us could sit on our asses and smoke weed all day long and became successful. Instead, most of us got out of bed—many times half asleep—pulled on our clothes and went to work, sometimes to a job we hated. We may have been up half the night caring for a sick child—it didn't matter—it was time for work.

We put ourselves on a tight budget and rarely went out to eat. We sweated, cried, and never gave up on what we believed in. We studied for our degree while working at job and reading textbooks and writing papers until midnight. We practiced something new until our fingers bled, our eyes were bloodshot, or our voices gave out. We drove the least expensive car we could find. Some of us figured out new uses for duct tape never tried before. We sucked it up and did what we needed to do.

When I started my new life at 32 years old, I had two part-time jobs. I was selling inexpensive women's shoes in a department store and men's shirts and accessories at another one. If those jobs hadn't come through, I was cued up to be a door-to-door vacuum cleaner salesman. Knock, knock. *"Hi, there! Can I come in and sell you a ridiculously expensive vacuum cleaner that you probably don't need?"*

At the time, I had a college degree, and a year earlier, I'd been the president of a nonprofit. Now I was selling women's shoes. Humiliating? Yeah, you could say so. But I did it to pay the rent, buy food, and put gas in the beat-up, faded, yellow Toyota Corolla I was driving, hoping nobody I knew saw me in it.

Bit by bit, year by year, my life came together. Some people believed in me and gave me a chance. I did the best I could with those opportunities and learned to keep going through all the ups and downs, of which there were many. My father's voice echoed in my head, *"Son, if you shake the tree, the apples will fall."* God, I hated that. What if the God damn tree doesn't have any apples, I asked? *"Find one that does."*

Creativity emerged from disappointment. Improvement followed failure. Confidence grew from embarrassment.

I'm well aware that what I've gone through is nothing compared to difficulties some people have experienced. But we all have our story, and sometimes the flame inside that makes us shine needs more air. If it does, it's a good time to remember what Snoop Dogg said in November 2018 when he received his Hollywood star.

After he thanked all the people that helped him in his life, he said,

> Last but not least, I wanna thank me
>
> I wanna thank me for believing in me
>
> I wanna thank me for doing all this hard work
>
> I wanna thank me for having no days off
>
> I wanna thank me for never quitting
>
> I wanna thank me for always being a giver
>
> And tryna give more than I receive

I wanna thank me for tryna do more right than wrong

I wanna thank me for just being me at all times

Snoop Dogg, you a bad motherf#%@#er.

You're right, Snoop. There are times when we don't give ourselves enough credit. So, pat yourself on the back today for being who you are and what you have accomplished. There's only one *you*, and you're amazing.

Be Yourself, Not Someone Else

You're just fine the way you are

When I was a little kid, I'd cry my eyes out whenever my mother read me the book, *The Little Rabbit Who Wanted Red Wings*. The rabbit wanted to be someone different, so he cast a spell on himself at a wishing pond and grew red wings. Returning home, his mother didn't recognize him and turned him away.

After a night of roughing it alone on the hard forest floor and crash-landing the next morning when he tried to fly, he finally realized he didn't want to be someone else. So, encouraged by a wise old groundhog, he went back to the wishing well, got rid of his wings, and returned home to the open arms of his mother.

It's a cute little story with a big message: Trying to be something you're not doesn't work. Deep down inside, we want to be who we are—a unique and perfect expression of our innate goodness and flaws.

Signs you might be growing red wings

You focus on pleasing others and ignore your own needs.

You struggle with setting personal boundaries.

You say Yes to virtually everything.

You're stressed out a lot.

You don't exercise enough, eat healthily, or get adequate and restful sleep.

You agree with other people in social settings to get along, even though you disagree.

You say one thing and do another.

You worry about what others think about you.

You don't know what you stand for.

You constantly compare yourself to others.

You spend inordinate amounts of time thinking about how to fit in.

Apparently, the challenge of being who you are isn't new. In the mid-1800s, Ralph Waldo Emerson wrote:

> *"To be yourself in a world that is constantly*
> *trying to make you something else*
> *is the greatest accomplishment."*

Being our authentic self is not always easy. We live in a world that bombards us with how we ought to look, dress, behave, and speak. Our perspective on life is shaped by when we grew up, where we've lived, our family of origin, our schooling, life experiences, our friends, and perhaps other influences. Along the way, we absorb messages about how to fit into our environment—what's acceptable behavior and what isn't.

The great marketing machine would like us to believe lasting happiness is found in being successful in our careers, making a lot of money, knowing the right people, what kind of car we drive, what part of town we live in, and so on. Beauty is portrayed by what we see on magazine covers and in the media. Now the wealthy are racing off into space apparently the latest frontier to conquer and prove themselves as pacesetters.

We get suckered into the rat race, and once we get in, it's hard to get out

I once coached a 40-year-old guy who had gotten himself deep in the matrix. He wanted to move up from being an individual contributor to being a manager. He pushed for a bigger opportunity, and it found him. Overnight he went from zero direct reports to 40. There was no "be a team leader first" where he could cut his teeth and learn the basics of leadership. He was thrown right into the fire.

He was working until midnight five days a week, barely sleeping, and making his wife and kids miserable. He believed doing a good job and building his career hung on his ability to keep up with everyone else to prove himself and impress his boss and colleagues. He was keen to find his calling, his niche in the world, but he worried that he wasn't making as much progress as his peers at his age. As a result, he started second-guessing what he said in meetings, fretting about what he should have said and what he didn't say.

He's grown little red wings

He asked me how he could have better boundaries. "You're working because you choose to work those hours," I told him. "How about choosing to stop working at a reasonable hour, for crying out loud, before you ruin your entire life?"

Working 18 hours a day is not some badge of honor to be proud of

Keeping up with the rat race looked good initially—the big title, the big paycheck, the big step up in the career. "It will look good on my CV," he said.

Not if you're dead, continually exhausted, or if your wife walks out," I replied.

There's nothing wrong with working hard to build a career, of course. It's the logical thing to do when you enter the workforce, and in particular, it's part of the maturation process as you move into midlife. During this "warrior phase" of life—from our 20s to our 50s, approximately—it's natural to compete in the world to prove our abilities and build our kingdom. I understand the situation he was in; I've been there, too. It's easy to buy into the mirage when trying to figure out who you are, what you stand for, and what you want to do.

It gets even more complex when you bring in the big question: "How do I find meaning and purpose in my life?" It's more complicated because if you assume that life's deeper treasures will be found in what you do for a living, it's easy to forget that finding meaning and purpose begins by discovering who you are on the inside.

For some, finding purpose and meaning is easy. For others, it emerges slowly as they mature. If some seem to be lagging behind, don't chase them down like they owe you money. Instead, find your purpose through understanding who you are and gain clarity about what you stand for and what's important to you.

Red wings can grow slowly, too. They're not obvious at first because we get so caught up in pursuing our hopes and dreams. We don't always notice when we're selling out. We're having fun, living life to its fullest. Each day is new and exciting; we're doing everything for the first time. We're on the big adventure. However, you don't want to grow red wings along the way. They'll eventually get in your way, and you'll likely crash land.

What you can do to ditch the red wings

¤ *Get clear on what you stand for.* Identify your core values and live by them. Values are your anchor, your guiding light, your North Star. If you aren't sure of your values, search the internet for a free assessment.

¤ *Ask yourself: "Am I staying true to myself in all that I do?"* When we're true to ourselves, we act in alignment with our highest values. If you have a lot of mental chatter about an issue, figure out what is important to you that is at risk. That's usually the trigger for mental unrest. Get in touch with what you care about, lean into it, and live by it. Don't compromise your values—ever.

¤ *Practice setting boundaries.* This means saying No to things you don't want to do and Yes to things you do. If you have difficulty doing this, ask a friend for help or hire a personal coach. Start with setting boundaries that don't stretch you too far. Build up to this slowly.

¤ *Practice saying No.* Learn to ask for what you want— directly. Too often, we drop hints or make suggestions. If people are left guessing what we want they are likely to ignore us. It's your birthright to ask for what you want. A request can be as simple as, "Can you please do X by tonight? "

¤ *Recognize your own goodness.* Worrying about what others think, trying too hard to fit in, and comparing yourself to others results from not loving and accepting yourself. Don't listen to any negative self-talk. Instead, reframe this with positive messaging. "I can deal with this." "I'm good." "I know how to do this." Living a life of peace begins with being forgiving, gentle, and kind to yourself. The world is tough enough. We all make mistakes; we're not perfect. We're flawed, and we're also fabulous.

¤ *Get in touch with your spiritual core.* You're not your thoughts or emotions—they're like passing clouds, coming and going. While they can be good informers, they're bad masters. Your real self is the silent mind, the awareness which looks through your eyes. Meditation can help get you in touch with your consciousness, your spiritual core. When you connect to your silent mind, you can more easily see your thoughts, emotions, and feelings because you become an observer. Meditation is like climbing a tower overlooking the landscape below. You get a clear view of what's in your environment.

> *"Be yourself; everyone else is already taken."*
> — OSCAR WILDE

¤ *Live above the line.* That means taking ownership and responsibility for the choices you make in life. Nobody makes you do anything (unless you are breaking a law!). You choose to behave as you do. There is no one else to blame. You have to play the cards you were dealt to the best of your ability. When you live below the line, you complain, blame others, and wish life has treated you differently. You grow red wings, and you become bitter and resentful.

*   *   *

Life is full of challenges. When we face one, we learn what's necessary for us at that time. There's no growth without them. It's like going to the gym. If we want to develop more strength, we choose exercises that challenge us. That's where the potential for growth is.

Lessons can come in different forms—some are operational, where we learn how to accomplish tasks or perform physical activities more effectively. Others help us learn more personal and private lessons about our inner world. The inner lessons are the most important.

As I've matured, I've come to realize that what I want is to live a peaceful life—a life of accepting who I am—the unique, one-of-a-kind me. The one without any red wings.

Inspiration to Stir Your Soul

Six sentences that always move me

S ome quotations inspire us for a few moments—or perhaps for a whole day. Some even inspire us for a lifetime. What Australian novelist Morris West wrote in his novel, *The Shoes of the Fisherman,* speaks to the reality of our existence with rich understanding, raw grit, and long-lasting inspiration. It's not sweet and gentle—it's a sledgehammer to your face. It blew me away the first time I read it 20 years ago, and it still does now.

> *"It costs so much to be a full human being. One has to abandon altogether the search for security and reach out to the risk of living with both arms. One has to embrace the world like a lover and yet demand no easy return of love. One has to accept pain as a condition of existence. One has to court doubt and darkness as the cost of knowing. One needs a will stubborn in conflict, but apt always to the total acceptance of every consequence of living and dying."*

Let's take this apart, line by line. What follows is my interpretation of what he means. You'll have yours.

It costs so much to be a full human being.

He gets my attention at the second word; he wants us to first ponder the cost. Then, he explains the price to pay in the following five lines. As for being a "full human being," here's my definition of "full": A state of being when you know you've done your best. You went for your dreams, pushed and stretched, soared and failed, left nothing out, dug deep, and were captivated by the mysteries of life and what's under the surface. You've tried to deal with your broken parts and make peace with your shadow. You walked away from following the norms and insidious unspoken rules stuffed down your throat by the system you've been in. You didn't take the easy way out of trouble— you took the road paved with choices that make you proud.

One has to abandon altogether the search for security and reach out to the risk of living with both arms.

You don't get to fullness by resisting doing the right thing just to be safe. Imagine you are a trapeze artist—you can't hold to what's not serving you with one arm while attempting to reach for what you really want with the other. That never works. You have to fully let go and move ahead with everything you've got. What's the risk of living with both arms? You might fail, fall, or be disappointed, but it's through failing that we learn and grow. That is the path to fullness. There's no other way.

One has to embrace the world like a lover and yet demand no easy return of love.

Lovers embrace full-on. They're all in. No holding back. No A-frame hugs. Invest all of yourself and release any expectation of what comes back, regardless of how much you put in. A lover doesn't ask for anything in return. A lover gives freely.

One has to accept pain as a condition of existence.

Birth into this world is painful. I watched the mother of my children give birth naturally on two occasions. She may not remember her screams, but I sure do. Through Holotropic Breathwork, I've relived my birth canal experience, and it was excruciatingly intense. Life has its painful times, and a great deal of mental and emotional suffering comes from wanting something other than what is happening to us in the moment. Accepting what we can't control allows us to find peace, even when we hurt. Pain is part of life and part of the journey to fullness.

One has to court doubt and darkness as the cost of knowing.

No matter how much you know now, you started in ignorance, knowing nothing. To learn, grow, and mature into a full human being, you pass through dark times. You learn to treat those times as your friend, not your enemy, because you know it's the price you pay for growth. You face fear and adversity without regret because you're committed to living life fully.

One needs a will stubborn in conflict, but always apt to the total acceptance of every consequence of living and dying.

You know what you stand for. You're a warrior, a champion for your humanity and the humanity of others. You fight like hell and play the game to win, knowing you might win or you might get outplayed and lose. But you don't let the results of your efforts define you because when you bring your heart, soul, and every bit of yourself to the party, you know you've done everything you could. And, when the party's over, you smile quietly to yourself, satisfied with how you played the game.

Live fully. Live with open arms. Accept what comes your way. Fight for what you believe in.

PART 2

Nurturing
the Inner World

How I Reclaimed My Life After
10 Years in a Cult

The road back to myself was paved with
sex, love, guns, and motorcycles

I never intended to join a cult when I was younger, but I did. My original plan was to get to know my inner self through meditation, but I was intrigued by the 14-year-old Indian prodigy "Guru Maharaji," now known as Prem Rawat, who spoke of creating world peace one person at a time.

I was inexplicably drawn to learn more about him and to become part of the growing movement of hippies, freaks, and spiritual seekers who were following him. I didn't want to dabble on the fringe. I wanted to go all in.

Prem Rawat is the youngest son of a guru from Northern India. When his father passed on in 1966, Prem, who was eight years old at the time, began addressing crowds of hundreds of thousands in India with a core message that has remained remarkably consistent over the past 50 years: "There is peace within, and I can help you experience it."

In the fall of 1972, my senior year in college, I learned how to practice his meditation techniques. My initial experience of meditation was low-key—peaceful and calming—but I kept at it for nine months more. My experience grew. I felt different. Something was happening within me, and I knew it was my path.

After graduating with a degree in English literature in 1973, I got involved in the organization that supported Mr. Rawat's activities in the United States. It was called Divine Light Mission at the time; it was a religious nonprofit. There were—and still are—millions of followers in India and 50,000 more internationally, but only a few hundred were direct employees that lived communally in ashrams and had taken vows of poverty, chastity, and obedience.

I took those vows. I took them because I wanted to understand everything I could about the experience of meditation and about this boy guru.

Life in the ashram

My life in the ashram began as a community leader. I soon became a meditation instructor and, eventually, the president of the organization, which was renamed Elan Vital. I started in Boston in 1973 and ended my work there in Miami in 1984. During those years, I traveled throughout the United States, Canada, Europe, Africa, and Australia.

I lived in ashrams —all were large, rented homes—with 10 to 12 other men and women known as brothers and sisters. We ate vegetarian food, sang devotional songs each morning, and meditated together. Some of us went off to regular jobs while others stayed behind in the ashram to do a variety of organizational tasks.

We ate dinner in silence, attended two-hour nightly meetings of music and inspirational talks, and then meditated more before bedtime. We slept on foam mattresses in shared rooms with two or three other roommates. It was frugal living, but we were happy—full of joy, love, and laughter. It was like living with a whole bunch of cool people taking a mild dose of MDMA every day—except we were sober. There was no sex, no drinking, no drugs, no visiting family, no movies, no TV, no bars, no restaurants. We received a minimal allowance each week but no salary or personal monies.

I lived like that for 10 years and believed I was following someone who could bring peace to the world. I was full of hope, happiness, and excitement. I was blissed out, utterly consumed with what I was doing.

My experience was reinforced by living and working with people who shared similar beliefs. We believed that Prem was the living "Perfect Master;" he could reveal perfection within. Many people referred to him as the "Lord of the Universe" or the *satguru*—the "true teacher" in Hindi. I drank the Kool-Aid in large quantities and became a true believer. Anyone who didn't subscribe to the belief that Mr. Rawat was the chosen one didn't get far in the organization.

Of course, I didn't think I was in a cult at the time. We worshipped Prem and treated him like a holy man and a celebrity. We gave him the best that money could buy. He lived on a multi-acre estate in Malibu and had other homes in Miami and London. Expensive cars, private aircraft, and helicopters were provided to him by his followers. Although there was never a fee to learn how to meditate, many people freely gave whatever they could. Some gave millions. Some gave their inheritances.

In India, it is not uncommon for followers to worship gurus as deities or lavish them with gifts, but in Western society, it's quite different. We expect our holy men or women to be chaste, modest, and unassuming. Mr. Rawat certainly broke those stereotypes when he left India at 13 and married an American woman four years later.

And yet, what he brought with him, reinforced by a close circle of former followers of his father, a guru himself, was the philosophy of Bhakti yoga, a spiritual practice within Hinduism that emphasizes devotion to a personal deity. Young Mr. Rawat embraced it and demanded unwavering devotion from his followers through the 1980s.

Moving into the inner circle

After becoming a meditation instructor with the organization, I traveled the world to teach meditation and speak at community gatherings. As a guest of honor, I was treated with a great deal of reverence. I received private rooms, personal drivers, cooked meals, and got my clothes washed and ironed. People attended to my every need; they hung on every word.

I felt enormous pressure to be an ever-present source of inspiration after months of traveling and speaking. It was a lonely life, too. I spent many days alone, as I spent my time reading, running, and listening to recordings of Prem speaking.

My sexual repression manifested in vivid, erotic dreams for years. Nobody ever spoke about sex, so I had no idea what others were experiencing. Eventually, I passed a message to Mr. Rawat about it, and he sent me a message back, telling me not to worry. It was natural, he said. That was somewhat helpful, but it certainly didn't take care of my raging hormones.

I always had a pleasant and loving but distant relationship with Prem. I think he filled a void in my life as a father figure, and I was grateful for what he taught me and the inspiration he provided. But as I learned more about his opulent lifestyle, I struggled to reconcile it with his public persona as an enlightened spiritual teacher. My intuition told me something was off but I pushed it aside until I had a chance to speak to him privately. When I asked him about his use of alcohol the first thing he said was, "Who told you?" I left the conversation less than satisfied but continued to march on with lingering doubts.

After touring the world for three years, Mr. Rawat asked me to become president of Elan Vital, and I said Yes. I moved into a large house with 10 others in an exclusive part of Miami Beach, and all of us worked in his legal and financial office. I had a private bedroom with a real bed, a car, a generous expense account, a secretary, and more access to Prem.

Dinner was no longer in silence. I caught up on movies I hadn't seen. I exercised more, drank non-alcoholic beer, wore expensive Italian suits and shoes (because Mr. Rawat did), and had a window into his private life. I was now close to the inner circle—and that circle was full of politics, drama, and privilege. I thought it would last forever, but it didn't.

A few years later, I started to date my secretary, and our relationship became a physical one. I spoke with Prem about it, and he said I could continue as president but should refrain from teaching meditation. He believed his meditation instructors should be celibate.

I continued as president until Mr. Rawat downsized Elan Vital, laying off 100 people and closing all of his ashrams worldwide. It was a messy process and could have been done with much more care. He also began redefining his public image from an Indian guru to a global peace ambassador. For me, the transition was many years too late but necessary to be more culturally acceptable. The 70s were well over, and the average person who might be interested in meditation would likely never get past the idea of worshipping a guru who demanded devotion to him. I also couldn't erase my memories of him in full Indian ceremonial garb, with a gold jeweled crown on his head, dancing on a massive stage in front of 10,000 devotees.

My secretary and I —we would eventually marry—were the last full-time staff to leave the house. I lined up a job selling business telephone systems. It was a bit of a shock: one day, I was the president of Elan Vital, and the next, I was a nervous salesperson knocking on doors in South Miami.

Life on the outside

I was dead broke. No money, no savings, not even a bank account. I borrowed $2,500 from a friend and began to build a new life with my wife. This included buying a car, furniture, and renting a one-bedroom condo. I was adjusting reasonably well to life on the outside, except that for the first six months I couldn't sleep through the night.

The stress of having sales targets to meet each week ravaged me. As a result, I was a mental and emotional wreck, a person suffering from a massive identity crisis.

A year later, I learned that Prem would be speaking at an event in Miami. I found myself standing in line for tickets and then sitting in the back of the venue. No one noticed or cared. Whoever I had been 12 months earlier didn't exist anymore. I had given my life to this movement for 10 years only to find myself just another follower, a stark reminder of what had always been the case.

In the years that followed, I struggled to find my foothold. My wife and I became parents. I stumbled through low-paid retail positions and found my way to other philosophies and ways of thinking. I spent hours in psychotherapy, found a path to heal many of the pains of my childhood, and was able to reconnect with my estranged father.

I started to play guitar again and began writing and recording songs. I got my ear pierced, got a couple of tattoos, and bought a Harley and a black leather jacket. I took long rides in the country and rode with the Vietnam vets down the freeway in Philadelphia.

I bought a Smith & Wesson Detective .38 special handgun—for no other reason than that I could. I got a permit to carry a concealed, loaded weapon and an underarm holster. I thought I was some kind of vigilante for a while. I wanted to do anything I couldn't do when I was in the ashram. I learned a lot about myself and what I was capable of, and I learned about my flaws and limitations.

My career had become very successful; my wife, children, and I gave people the impression of the perfect American family. But, inside, I was struggling, and it manifested in self-destructive behaviors, including a short-lived affair and a prescription drug dependency. Eventually, my marriage came apart. The guilt about breaking up the family haunted me for years, even though the divorce was amicable, and we remained good friends. It didn't stop until I could establish a new peaceful life of self-acceptance.

I wanted to integrate aspects of myself I had kept hidden for so many years—my insecurities, self-doubt, and risk-taking behavior. I realized that accepting them did not diminish my strengths and gifts but made me a more complete human being. As I did so, I became more forgiving of myself and others.

I thought about Prem—groomed to be a guru as a child, worshipped by millions at eight years old, and gaining vast power and wealth as a teenager. It was hard for me to imagine the psychology of being raised as a child god. While he had incredible gifts and talents, I began to see him as a person with imperfections, just like the rest of us.

Yet, my eyes opened even wider in 2001 when I read online blogs written by his closest advisor revealing more details about inappropriate behavior. And since then, more facts have emerged about his character that I found unacceptable for an alleged spiritual leader. I cut my ties with him completely.

Over the past few years, I've wondered how deep and long-lasting the psychological impact of worshipping another human being is, particularly when you're as young as I was. I've wondered about my motivations to get so involved and the interplay of free choice and destiny. I've wondered how my beliefs about him were shaped. I've wondered how I can reclaim the personal power I gave away during the years I was at the ashram.

Apparently, the psychological impact does run deep because I'm 70 now, and I'm still dealing with it 50 years later. I've had to do my untangling, and it hasn't been easy. Perhaps Prem has done his. Maybe that's why he's now a global peace ambassador and not the "Perfect Master" anymore.

Through the eyes of resolution

Throughout my time with Divine Light Mission and Elan Vital, I saw some beautiful parts of our planet. In my 20s, I worked with people from many cultures and countries. I experienced first-hand that human beings everywhere want inner peace, whether they're in a small village in Africa or in central Vienna. I developed the confidence and ability to speak in public, a skill that has served me well. I learned about service, humility, and kindness and made many lifelong friends.

I witnessed the great things people can accomplish when they have a shared purpose and mission. I learned about simplicity—and I learned that I don't need much to live and be happy.

Of course, there was a price to pay for immersing myself as I did. I got a late start with my psychological maturity. I didn't understand how to be in intimate relationships. I repressed my sexuality, which played itself out in a variety of unhealthy manifestations. I developed a spiritual ego and viewed spirituality through the narrow lens of life as a monastic, which has taken many years to dismantle.

* * *

I have no regrets. The inner experience I had—and still have—is incredible. My life during those 10 years made me what I am today—flaws and all—and I wouldn't change a thing. It was my path.

Happiness Comes from Learning
to Play the Inner Game

Lessons for a life well-lived

I stared out the window as we passed the Ridgewood, New Jersey train station. Commuters—all men with overcoats, suits, and briefcases—stood on the platform, waiting for the train to New York like a herd of clones. I thought, *"Not for me. There's got to be more to life than that. I'll be blazing my own trail."* It was the 1960s, and my dad was driving teenaged me to high school.

That was my first moment of inner awakening. I knew what I *didn't* want, but I still had no idea what I *wanted*—or how to go about figuring it out. As I've already described, I went full counterculture, living in an ashram for 10 years before eventually finding my way into a successful career in corporate America.

Two games—the inner and outer

I learned that finding my way consisted of understanding there were two games to play. One was the *inner game*—knowing my inner self, defining what I stood for, connecting to spirit, and breaking free from limiting beliefs. The other was the *outer game*—focusing on what I did in life and how I behaved. The way I played the outer game reflected how I played the inner game. I'll go into greater detail about both games later, but for now, I want to talk about winning—in both games.

I realized the only way to succeed in the *outer* game was to put as much effort into the *inner* game—connecting with spirit, knowing our true self—as possible. The more I did that, the more I enjoyed the outer game and the less stressful it became. Meditation, mindfulness, neuroscience, diet, health, exercise, and visualization improved my inner game.

Carl Jung once said, "The first half of life is devoted to forming a healthy ego; the second half is going inward and letting go of it." I think he had it partially right. In the first part of adult life, we build our careers, prove ourselves, and develop a strong sense of self. But no matter how old we are or how long the second half of life is, learning to play the inner game will only enhance our experience and help us be even more successful.

I've leaned on the following five lessons many times since then. They've helped me play the inner game through the good times and the bad.

1. Be response-able

We can choose our response to any situation. We're not accountable for things others do or say; we're responsible for our behavior.

There is a direct connection between empowerment and being responsible for our actions. Someone who has stepped into their power doesn't complain or blame others. They know the ball is always in their court, and they accept the cards they've been dealt. Focus on what's in your control. There's no point in wasting time and energy on things you can't do anything about. We always think we're in control—until we realize we aren't.

2. Maintain a learning mindset

Learning anything new is difficult and can be both frustrating and humiliating. I've fallen on my face many times. I've blown sales calls, presentations, and speeches. I've been so embarrassed I wanted to crawl off somewhere and never return. After some soul searching, I realized the way back in the game is to focus on getting better and letting go of the past. Focus on learning—not looking good or being right. We can only learn and grow when we are curious. I learned the most about curiosity when I was thrown into a job way over my head. I went into survival mode—all I could do was learn as quickly as I could. I had to accept how much I didn't yet know and embrace the opportunity to learn. A curious mind knows it doesn't know everything.

When we have a learning mindset, we're naturally more resilient. We want to figure out how to recover, we're curious to understand what we don't know, and we can adapt more easily because we're flexible.

3. Keep your heart open

Even though I've always been a planner and a list-maker, I've also tried to live from my heart. I've followed my instincts and passions, and it's helped me immensely. The energy and happiness I received from investing in my heart have been profound.

My meditation practice has been central to keeping my heart open. No matter what, the inner experience, that beautiful world inside each of us, has never let me down. It's been a constant source of inner fulfillment despite any chaos around me. The kinder we are to ourselves, the more kindness and understanding we can extend to others.

4. Tell your truth

We suffer when we don't speak our truth, and we flourish when we do. A dear friend once told me that we have to be willing to disappoint others when we speak our truth. Our experience, what is true for us, is powerful. It can inspire, inform, and ignite change. I've learned not to sacrifice my truth to appease others. Every person is entitled to their opinion because we all see the world differently. But problems occur when people think their opinion is fact and impose it on others.

When I express my opinion as just my view, it's powerful and engaging because it invites dialogue. Presenting my opinion as a fact creates defensiveness. If you have an opinion or a point of view, share it confidently and appropriately. But don't expect agreement from others. Their journey is their own, and it won't be on the same path as yours.

5. Notice and manage your patterns of thought

As author Mike Dooley says, a fundamental principle of the inner game is that our thoughts become things. Our self-talk influences our language, behavior, and mental and physical health. I've experienced significant personal breakthroughs as a direct result of changing my thinking patterns.

There is plenty of research regarding the human capacity to rewire our brains. One way to start is to observe our thoughts, emotions, and feelings. They're here to inform us, not to run our lives.

The simple act of noticing thought patterns initiates change. When you notice a thought, you can change it, but you can't change something if you haven't taken the time to notice it.

*   *   *

On a cold November morning in Philadelphia, shortly after I left the ashram and had started my job teaching sales training, I found myself in a suit and tie, with an overcoat and a briefcase in each hand, waiting for a train to take me to work. Sound familiar? I was happy to have a decent job, my wife was pregnant with our first child, and we were pretty broke. I looked like every other guy standing on the platform. I smiled at the irony and thought maybe some kid would see me and decide to go blaze their own trail, too. I hope so.

The Real Reason
We Get into Arguments . . .

What I learned after a stupid meltdown

I want to tell you a story. I'm not proud of my behavior; in fact, it's downright embarrassing to tell you what I did. But it was a wake-up call that stirred things up for the better. Believe me, I don't always have such a short fuse.

I was watching my 12-year-old son play in a tennis tournament. The kids were playing for rankings, which would determine scholarship offers for college tennis over the next few years. (You could say there was money on the table.) A cellphone went off near me. Phones were supposed to be silenced. I looked over and saw that the phone belonged to Alan, the father of one of the kids. He answered the phone and had a brief conversation. I shot him a dirty look. It rang again. Now I was really annoyed.

"Hey, you know the rules. Turn your phone off," I said.

Alan retorted, "I need to take these calls."

"Put it on silent then."

"It's no big deal. What do you think this is—Wimbledon or something?"

"It doesn't matter. Turn your phone off."

"But I'm a doctor."

"A doctor?" I thought. *"Are you fucking kidding me? You just poured gas on the fire. You want to do battle? Let's go!"*

"I don't give a fuck who you are. It's disturbing to the kids. Be respectful."

"Nobody speaks to me that way."

"Really? Well, too fucking bad."

By this time, someone had intervened and told us both to cool off. Alan puttered around behind me, talking to himself. I got up and walked outside for a few minutes and then finally returned. No one said another word. My son finished his match, and we left.

A month later, I was at another tournament. I saw Alan's wife, and she smiled and waved at me. I was surprised. *She's not upset?* I walked over to say hello.

"Did Alan tell you about the incident at the last tournament?" I asked her.

"No. Why?" she asked.

"We had a little problem." I told her the story. She didn't seem surprised.

"I'm so sorry. He's not a doctor. He's an out-of-work stockbroker, and he's, well, a bit depressed and on medication. He's quite hard to deal with these days."

"Well, tell him I apologize for going off."

"He probably deserved it, but I'll tell him."

It made me wonder how I would have handled things if I had known he wasn't doing well. I would much rather it have gone like this: "Excuse me, could you please turn off your phone?"

"But I'm a doctor."

"I see. Could you please put it on vibrate and take calls elsewhere so you don't disturb the kids?"

Maybe he still would have stamped his feet. If I didn't curse at him, at least I would have known I behaved respectfully. Henry Wadsworth Longfellow once said, "Every man has his secret sorrows which the world knows not, and oftentimes we call a man cold when he is only sad."

It wasn't long before Alan and I met up at another tournament. We nodded politely at each other. No words were spoken. His son was playing with my son. We stood near each other for the next few hours. No cellphones rang. His son went on to beat mine, and I congratulated him on the victory. A few years later, both boys went on to play college tennis at major universities. Everybody was happy.

It's painful to look back and see my younger self losing his temper over a ringing cellphone. But here's what I didn't realize at the time: I was carrying my wounds, too.

My first wife and I were going through a divorce. While it was mostly amicable, my dream of a nuclear family living together was blowing up. I was guilt-stricken, depressed, and financially worried. I kept this mainly to myself, carrying on as best I could, assuming I could handle everything by just marching on like it didn't exist.

If I could turn back time and give myself some advice, this is what I would say:

- ¤ Realize you are going through a monumental life transition.
- ¤ Pay attention to your emotional state of mind.
- ¤ Take care of yourself.
- ¤ Slow down and give yourself time to heal.
- ¤ Lower your expectations; you're not superman.
- ¤ The suffering will affect you.
- ¤ Find someone to talk to.

Too often when I have gone through a personal crisis I've paid more attention to what's going on around me and not enough to what's going on in me. My focus was on my work, my kids, and my relationships. Assuming my psyche would magically heal on its own without giving it any attention was foolish.

It's so easy to get lost in ourselves, in our world, and be consumed by the pressures of our lives. Some of us bottle it up, not even aware we're doing it. And then there's a trigger. The anger and self-hatred come pouring out all over someone else.

Funny how two grown men at their kids' tennis tournament can stir up each other's trauma in such destructive ways. Are we somehow drawn to each other's wounds, silently hoping for the healing we don't even realize we need? When Alan's cellphone rang at the tournament that day, I never considered what he might be going through, what wounds were haunting him. But it turns out we both were reeling from invisible wounds.

It's quite normal for us to look past our wounds, not wanting to lose the connection to the sense of self we've created. We've worked hard to be who we think we are; recognizing a reality that deviates from that is even harder work. Our self-identity and our face to the world are our closest friends, allies, and protectors. They have been with us through our ups and downs. We've come to rely on our inner voice for guidance and help. Sometimes it comforts us. Sometimes it tortures us with guilt and shame. But it's all we know, so we hold onto it tight.

I've been hard on myself throughout my life. I've pushed and fought hard to accomplish things and get through the hard times. My high-achieving, perfectionist tendencies covered up deep insecurities and wounds, and for many years I didn't know how to face the wounded part of myself. But I've come to appreciate that life sometimes opens doors for us, and if we are brave enough to walk through, we can face our demons and make peace with them.

The more I began to accept my dark side, the more I learned the path to wholeness is paved with accepting and loving myself—all parts: my gifts and power, my darkness and weakness. As a result, I believe when we are more kind and loving to ourselves, we can be more tolerant and forgiving of others.

For me, opening and walking through that door led me to my true self—a small, frightened kid who found his way into adulthood and did the best he could. He's made many mistakes and failed at many things, but he's learning that acceptance of others begins with accepting himself.

*   *   *

We're all a bit broken in some way or another. Wouldn't the world be a much better place if we accepted it and recognized that everyone is working through their wounds, trying to find their way home? If we did, I bet we'd show each other a little more understanding, forgiveness, and compassion.

How to Face Your Limiting Beliefs
and Transform Your Life

To live the life you want,
first look at what's holding you back

A belief is something we acccpt as truc without proof. Beliefs are powerful. We look through them like they're a clean window, not always noticing them, but they're there just the same. Beliefs give us hope, meaning, and safety in an unpredictable world, but they can also sabotage us.

In 2016, I was a successful sales executive living comfortably in suburbia. I was quite satisfied with most of my life. I had engaging hobbies good friends, and traveled to exciting places for my job. In my marriage, however, I knew something was missing.

The relationship had gone flat years before. Tolerance and convenience crept in, replacing real caring and genuine love. My unhappiness leaked out in criticism and complaints; hers came out in bursts of anger and "I can't take this anymore!"

I went to a cryotherapy office to get treatment for my injured knee. A man overheard my conversation with the therapist about my knee and stopped to ask if he could speak to me.

"From a mind/body connection point of view," he said, "your knees represent your ability to move forward. Here's my card. If you'd like to discuss it more, give me a call."

In that moment, I realized more was going on with my body—my life!—than a simple knee injury. The man was right: I was stuck. I was not moving forward. It was time to listen to what my body was telling me.

Brian, a health and wellness coach, carefully listened as I told him that I was afraid to have an honest conversation with my wife. I was afraid of what undoing a 10-year relationship would mean. He asked me to write down three beliefs about my current situation.

I took out a piece of scrap paper and wrote: "I don't deserve everything. I'm afraid of what might happen. I'm content with 'it's good enough.'"

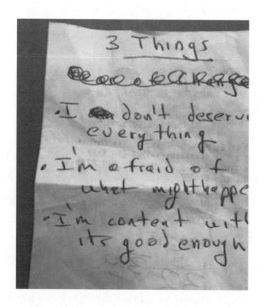

When I looked at what I had written on that scrap of paper, I realized that those beliefs were running my life.

"I don't deserve everything."

Well, that's a real deal-killer. I won't ever have what I want if I continue with that attitude. I concluded that I deserve *everything*—everything that is possible for me and everything that will allow me to have a great life. That means living peacefully and happily and having a loving relationship, good health, engaging, meaningful work, and secure finances.

"I'm afraid of what might happen."

I had convinced myself that only negative circumstances would come from ending my marriage: My wife will get upset. A divorce will be messy. I won't have enough money. But not one of those things ever happened. I had only convinced myself that they would—because of fear.

"I'm content with 'it's good enough.'"

I'd given up on the possibility of having a loving and connected relationship. I've never been a person who settles, but there I was, accepting what I had even though I knew it wasn't what I wanted.

I knew I had to make a change and stop letting those limiting beliefs dictate my life. The conversation with my wife wasn't nearly as difficult as I imagined it to be. She understood and supported me. Even if we weren't meant to be together, we both still cared for each other and wanted each other to have full, meaningful lives. We separated, began a process of mediation, and soon divorced.

I learned a great deal from that experience. That wisdom stays with me; I've used it ever since. Here are five principles that helped me.

1. Do the inner work

By acknowledging my three unconscious beliefs, I brought them up from my subconscious mind into my everyday awareness. I understood how they'd been the lens I'd been looking through, but I hadn't been aware of how they were limiting me. That awareness began the transformation process. I found the humility and the drive within me to ask for help, putting me at the threshold of significant change.

I took long reflective walks and spent time with a therapist. I had to face the dark side of my personality—a part I didn't want to admit was there. I'd kept it at a distance, that secret, guilt-ridden side of me, by saying to myself, *"I'm better than that. I'll ignore it, and it will go away."* The simple act of beginning to learn acceptance made a big impact on my feelings of self-worth and dignity.

2. Use the power of visualization and affirmations

Visualization and affirmations are recognized practices that help manifest intentions and goals. Successful athletes and other successful people have used visualization techniques to improve performance for years. I have practiced visualizations and affirmations for a few years, and I have seen the results. My life is filled with more richness and peace than ever before.

During my 10-year marriage, I discovered what I really wanted in a relationship—and what I didn't. *"I want a strong, powerful, loving woman who knows herself and is connected to spirit."* I was visualizing what I wanted without being aware of it!

3. Define and live your values

I've identified my four core values as integrity—being proud of my behavior; responsibility—owning the choices I make; humility—having a curious mindset; and respect for others—kindness.

When I overlooked my values, my inner peace suffered. Living in alignment with my values brought me much-needed satisfaction and contentment. No matter what happens, my values are my foundation and anchor.

4. Recognize the importance of connection

The fundamental breakdown in my marriage was a lack of connection. While my wife and I enjoyed many things together—cooking, sex, socializing, traveling—we didn't share spiritual camaraderie. For many couples, this might not be an issue. For me, it was an essential part of connection. I overlooked its importance when we got married, and that was my mistake.

In the absence of a meaningful connection, I developed addictive behaviors that didn't serve me well. To overcome them, I needed to find the connection I wanted in life.

5. Be patient but don't give up

For a while, I was frustrated with myself for not doing anything to change my situation; but now I realize I couldn't have made a change until I was ready. I had to hit bottom. I had to find the motivation within me to do something. When I accepted reality, instead of rationalizing it all away, I opened myself to the possibility of making the change.

Recognizing my false beliefs, acknowledging the power they have over my life, and working to change them was not easy. But I had to trust myself that I was ready, and with a little nudge from Brian—and my body—I was.

Not long after my divorce, I traveled to Scotland on business. At a company meeting, I sat at a table with four people, one of whom was a woman I did not know. During a break, she and I struck up a conversation. I told her my story, and she smiled. I learned that she had been on her own journey since her divorce and had just completed a women's ceremony two days before, asking her guides, spirits, and angels to send her the man she needed.

As she spoke, I found myself gazing into the eyes of a powerful, loving woman grounded in self-knowledge and spirit. I was home. She was Mariclaire, now my wife.

*   *   *

Mariclaire and I now live in a small village in northeast Scotland. We continue to learn how to be better lovers and better humans—with each other and with the world around us. While the journey here wasn't easy, I'm deeply thankful I was able to let go of my limiting beliefs and have the life I had once thought was impossible.

You can do so, too.

The Stories You Tell Yourself
Make or Break You

Misery begins and ends in your head

I n July 2020, Mariclaire and I were sitting in our back garden, a small fire burning in front of us, smoke curling up, the earthy smell of peat hanging in the cool air. I looked up at the stars and planets sparkling bright in the clear, pitch-black evening sky. A peaceful feeling wrapped me like a warm blanket. I felt so good.

After about an hour, Mariclaire said she wanted to go inside. Seconds after she left, my mind kicked in: *"Why is she going in? She should stay out here with me. If we were on a date, she wouldn't just get up and leave. Not very romantic of her. Maybe she doesn't love me like she used to."*

I felt the air slowly leak out of my tires; the beautiful peace slowly dissolved into a subtle disturbance. I took the simple fact that she went inside, and I unconsciously made up a story about it.

I also remembered the work of former Harvard professor Chris Argyris who explained how our brains selectively take in data, add meaning, and form conclusions and beliefs in milliseconds. He captured this neurological process in a model he called the "Ladder of Inference."

It's easy to make assumptions and false interpretations. Our brains do it automatically, wanting to finish what they consider incomplete stories.

When someone we know ignores us when they pass by, we complete the story by thinking they're aloof or avoiding us. When someone doesn't promptly answer an email, we assume they don't care about us. When our boss calls us to a meeting unexpectedly, we think the worst. These might be problematic to a degree, but the real problems occur when we act on our incorrect inferences and false stories. Who among us hasn't caught themselves assuming something about someone, only to later realize we were completely wrong?

Argyris' theory also applies to what happens when our made-up stories become beliefs. Anna Pease, the senior editor at Management Consulted, said:

> "Once you form strong beliefs, you may find yourself increasingly selecting data that ends up reinforcing those very same beliefs. This is the "reflexive loop." It leads you to quickly move up the ladder toward decisions and actions that seem very fact-based. But in reality, they are ultimately a function of the beliefs you had before even considering the objective facts of the situation."

LADDER OF INFERENCE

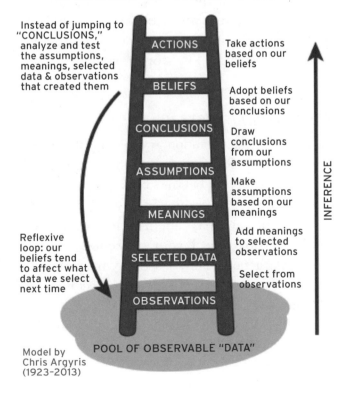

Instead of jumping to "CONCLUSIONS," analyze and test the assumptions, meanings, selected data & observations that created them

ACTIONS — Take actions based on our beliefs

BELIEFS — Adopt beliefs based on our conclusions

CONCLUSIONS — Draw conclusions from our assumptions

ASSUMPTIONS — Make assumptions based on our meanings

MEANINGS — Add meanings to selected observations

SELECTED DATA — Select from observations

Reflexive loop: our beliefs tend to affect what data we select next time

OBSERVATIONS

INFERENCE

Model by Chris Argyris (1923-2013)

POOL OF OBSERVABLE "DATA"

Pease's reflexive loop theory helps explain why it's difficult for people to let go of firmly held beliefs and biases: We find what we focus on.

Imagine that someone you know has a reputation for being obnoxious at social gatherings. People will be on the lookout for that person's bad behavior. If someone is consistently quiet in team meetings, those who think that person is disengaged will look for evidence of disengagement. Strong political views are strengthened by selectively choosing facts that support a particular belief.

We find what we focus on

When we hold onto false stories and act on them, those stories can transform us from bright, happy people, full of all life's goodness, to bitter, resentful, and powerless souls. An event occurs, we attach meaning to the event, take it personally, or create a false negative story, and before we know it, we're miserable and can't find our way out.

But it doesn't have to be that way. If we recognize the false story, we can set ourselves free. The stories we tell ourselves make or break us.

Using the ladder of inference

When you make an interpretation, try to make it the most respectful interpretation—or "MRI"—that you can. Err on the side of assuming good intentions. Try: "I bet she's busy and just forgot to book the order. I'll send her a friendly reminder" instead of "She never answers her emails" or "She never pays attention to my requests."

Whenever possible, check your inferences before you form a conclusion or take action. "Hey, based on what you said in the meeting, I'm thinking that you don't think the project I'm working on will pan out. Is that correct?"

Ask yourself, "What don't I know about this situation? Why did I make this assumption? Is my conclusion based on facts?"

When speaking, make sure people understand your thinking and reasoning. Walk them *up the ladder* by telling them what you think and why. Make it easy for them to understand your thought process, your conclusions, and your beliefs.

When listening to someone who isn't explaining their reasoning, ask them to do so. Walk them *down the ladder* by asking questions: "Okay, I see you believe we need to change our customer acquisition strategy. Please help me understand your reasoning and the facts behind your decision."

Most importantly, be aware of your thought process. Notice what judgments, interpretations, and beliefs you hold.

* * *

Sitting in the garden, I replayed the facts in my head: *Mariclaire said she wanted to go inside, then she got up and left. That's it. Those are the pure facts.* Before I went all the way "up the ladder," I caught myself and let go of the story I'd made up. As soon as I did, peace flooded back into my being. I breathed deeply.

It was getting late, and the fire was burning down. I stood up and walked back into the house. Mariclaire was in the kitchen.

"Hey, babe. I just wanted to clean up this mess before we hop into bed."

I chuckled to myself. She had gone inside to wash the dishes.

How to Weather the Storm in Your Head

To conquer negative thoughts,
think of yourself on a hero's journey

L ife is full of challenges. We never know what's coming our way until it shows up. How we handle difficult situations, uncertainty, and stress can make the difference between an enjoyable life and one that always seems to be spinning out of control.

So let's take a look at how cows and buffalo handle adversity!

In Colorado, cows and buffalo live relatively close together because of the area's unique topography. The Rocky Mountains are in the western and middle parts of the state, and vast plains lie to the east. When a storm rolls in from the west, grazing cows run east with the storm. Cows can run, but not fast, so they don't outrun the bad weather at all. They get stuck in it, subject to the very thing they are trying to avoid.

Buffalo, however, charge directly into a storm. They move through it more quickly, minimizing the amount of time they spend suffering.

So, how do we learn from the buffalo and move into and through a storm?

See adversity as a challenge

Imagine you're on a crowded bus or subway. You feel someone standing on your foot. What do you do? You could suffer silently and complain to yourself, or you could accept the problem is yours and figure out the best way to deal with it.

Consider the pandemic. We wanted our cities and towns opened back up; we wanted our lives to be the way they were before. We might have been angry, frustrated, depressed, worried, financially at risk, or we might just have been annoyed and bored. If we believe we can't do anything to improve our situation, we'll find ourselves behind an immovable obstacle. We end up being powerless. But if we see our situation as a challenge, then the game changes. We start to think about what we can do.

Author and psychiatrist Dr. Viktor Frankl faced death every day in the Nazi concentration camps during WWII. Frankl coined the phrase "tragic optimism," which he described as "the human capacity to creatively turn life's negative aspects into something positive or constructive."

I don't like what happened during the pandemic, and I didn't create it, but its impact on me is my problem. I only have so many breaths left, and I'm not going to waste them complaining and being miserable about what I cannot change. I'm committed to doing the best that I can in this new world, and I will face the storm like a badass buffalo.

Accept that you are now on a learning journey

We go through a very predictable, archetypal pattern during times of change. Understanding this pattern can help bring meaning to chaos. The hero's journey, which Joseph Campbell describes in his book, *Hero with a Thousand Faces*, explains the universal pattern of stability, crisis, introspection, growth, and restoration of order. Stories throughout the ages—and in Hollywood movies such as *The Lord of The Rings, Star Wars, The Matrix*, and *The Lion King*—follow this formula.

For example, in the *Lion King*, Simba, the young lion hero, survives an attempt on his life by wicked uncle Scar. His father does not survive, and Simba leaves the kingdom for the jungles and enters a time of mourning, chaos, and self-discovery. When he finally accepts his own power as the future king, he returns to the kingdom, faces and kills Scar, and restores order.

The Hero's Journey

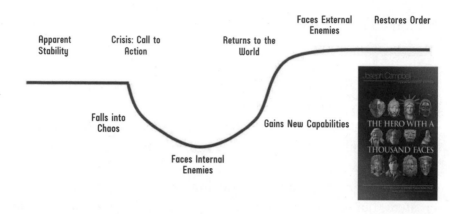

In early 2020, there was a relative degree of social stability. Then the Covid virus hit, and our society entered into a period of chaos. There we began our journey, and from time to time we met a formidable enemy—inner resistance to the "new normal." Think of something you can do easily but you had to learn how to do it. Perhaps it is golf, knitting, painting, or playing a musical instrument. It might have been difficult to do at first, and then it became easier. Right now, we are all learning how to play a new game in our lives. It's not comfortable.

We are all on a hero's journey, whether we know it or not. Understanding it helps us realize that:

- ¤ Our experience is universal; you aren't alone.
- ¤ We are making progress, even if it seems like we aren't. The destination is learning and growth.
- ¤ We need to be patient with ourselves and keep making smart choices. We create our inner world by giving credence to some thoughts and not others. We need to carefully choose the good ones.

Reframe negative thoughts

Lao Tzu said, "Watch your thoughts; they become your words. Watch your words; they become your actions. Watch your actions; they become your habits. Watch your habits; they become your character. Watch your character; it becomes your destiny."

Our thoughts influence our behavior. By paying attention to our inner world—our thoughts, feelings, and emotions—we can choose where we put our focus. For example, if I say that I'm in "lockdown" due to the pandemic, the negative implications of that jail-like mentality are loss of control, helplessness, removal of dignity, poverty, and more. But what if I can reframe that statement and the underlying belief? I'm not in lockdown; I'm spending more time with my family. I might have more time to do more research and writing; I might now have time to prepare myself for my next job; I might be doing my part to keep myself and others safe.

Markham Heid writes about the importance of cognitive reframing in his article, "How to Take Control When You're Emotionally Overwhelmed." He says, "Cognitive reframing is a major component of cognitive-behavioral therapy (CBT)—now widely considered the gold standard in psychotherapy—and it involves challenging and changing the underlying thoughts that give rise to unhelpful emotions."

We can let go of false stories, assumptions, limiting beliefs, and self-doubt. We create our inner world by giving credence to some thoughts and not others. Choose good ones.

Meditate

I begin every day with at least 20 minutes of quiet meditation. I close my eyes and tune into my breath, observing it flow in and out. Observing the breath reminds me that the peace and satisfaction I so often seek outside of me are within. When so little is in my control in the world around me, having an inner source of tranquility is truly a gift. There are many excellent and free tools that can help us meditate. There are many online videos, classes, and apps available. For me, the foundation for managing *the inside game* is meditation. It's a proven way to increase focus, gratitude, and resilience. That's why I've been doing it for about five decades.

Know what game you're playing

Ask yourself: What game am I playing? What are the rules? Who wins and loses? You can also use these questions as a check-in with your family, friends, and co-workers. It's a great non-threatening way to launch a rich conversation.

So, what game *are* you playing? Are you going to be sick and tired of the bullshit and want it over and done with so you can continue in your bad mood? Or are you going to connect with friends and spread positive energy? Are you going to find peace with whatever you do?

*   *   *

You're in a power-*full* game if you're thinking about what challenge you are facing, what your past experience has taught you, and how you can use it to respond. You're in a power-*less* game if you're thinking about why what's happening is being done *to* you and that they should not have done this. It takes courage to face a storm, be power-full, and manage the inside game.

The Difference Between
Winning and Succeeding

Nothing beats aligning with your values

My heart was pounding—it wasn't a good sign. I opened my mouth, and it felt chalky. I needed water, lots of it. My mind was freezing up, too. The mouths of the four people interviewing me were moving, but I couldn't process what they were saying. Panic swallowed me up. I stumbled my way through the next 20 minutes. It couldn't end soon enough.

When the disaster was over, one guy pulled me aside and asked me how I thought the interview had gone. *"How does 'terrible' sound?"* I thought. I mumbled something about involving everyone in the discussion and some other nonsense. I asked him what he thought, and he said, "We'll get back to you."

Then he smiled and said, "Thanks for coming in. Have some lunch before you go." I thought I heard him say, "Don't let the door hit you on the way out, you loser," but that was probably just another hallucination I invented, along with the one that told me that if I got the job, I'd be all set in life. I dragged myself to the airport and flew home, replaying the debacle over and over in my mind. Weeks of preparation had just gone up in flames.

No safety net

This little tragedy happened during the financial recession in 2010. I had been laid off after four years with a startup and living on unemployment checks. I'd already been turned down a dozen times in my job search before a recruiter called me with a particular sales opportunity that ended in my worst-ever performance in an interview. It had sounded great at first—an exciting job, good money, and a trustworthy company. I had a strong background in sales and knew

71

people who worked in the company. The odds looked pretty good, and I wanted the job.

The interview process was rigorous. First, an IQ test, a personality assessment, and the first part of a sales simulation followed by a half-day face-to-face interview with four execs. I studied, took preparatory IQ tests, and worked my butt off for several weeks.

When the big day finally arrived, I sat at one end of a large conference table, looking at the people who would decide my fate. I promptly choked.

When I returned home, the recruiter called.

"Sorry. They're going to pass on you."

"Oh, really? I can't imagine why," I thought.

"Any feedback?" I asked.

"They said you weren't listening to what they were saying during the simulation."

Wow. Sales 101. Wasn't listening? He was damn right I wasn't listening. I was frozen, flooded, hijacked by my amygdala, panicked, and scared I would fail.

After the call, I sat back in my chair. Scared to fail? Why would I be scared to fail?

Well, I had plenty to worry about. I was on unemployment, which was ending soon. I'd run out of money and have to drain my savings. I wouldn't be able to find another job. I'd be dumpster-diving for food.

I knew it was fear talking, so I worked hard over the next few weeks to let it go. I also knew I failed during the interview process because I wanted that damn job more than my cat wanted food in the morning. I had a goal, but I had no inner safety net to catch me if I didn't achieve it, and I got myself hooked on something I couldn't control.

The big money, title, and imagination of how wonderful life would have been with that particular job seduced me. I even had a new car picked out. I forgot one essential thing: We can choose our actions, but we can't choose the result of our efforts. I neglected to make the distinction between "winning" and "succeeding."

Winning

Winning is the result of accomplishing a goal: getting the job you want, beating someone in tennis, securing a new customer. But we can't always control outcomes. Hiring managers decide who gets hired. I can play my very best in a tennis match and still lose because someone else played better. Customers choose who they want to work with; suppliers don't.

When our happiness is tied to conditional results, we're at risk of disappointment, fear, and anxiety. We suffer needlessly, attached to something we can't have. Only in our minds do we control what isn't ours.

When we face life's challenges, we need something within our control that gives us support and that builds courage, resiliency, and confidence.

Success

Success is not about winning. Success is a result of behaving in alignment with our highest values without being attached to the outcome of our actions. For me, success is:

¤ Being proud of my behavior.

¤ Conducting myself so there's nothing to second-guess at the end of the day.

¤ Doing my best, focusing my efforts on what can produce the best possible outcome, and knowing full well I can't dictate the results.

¤ Performing as best I can and celebrating the winner—no matter who it is.

¤ Telling my kids at night how I did the right thing, not how I did everything right.

¤ Fully investing myself in something without the expectation of an easy return.

Success is your safety net. It protects you from the torture of self-criticism, second-guessing, fear of failure, and embarrassment. It offers you universal support, strength, self-esteem, and peace of mind. It helps create a mindset of learning, growth, and being a better version of yourself.

Success is based on knowing what is within your control. There are only four things in your control:

¤ Your mindset: your values, attitudes, and beliefs

¤ What you say: the words you choose

¤ How you say it: tone of voice, emotions, body language

¤ How you behave: the choices you make and your actions

Success manifests in how we behave. Our mindset influences our behavior, and one component of our mindset is our values, that is, what we stand for. Values are principles and standards of behavior. When you know what you stand for, you can make smarter choices about what you say and how you behave.

I have four fundamental values:

¤ Response-ability: the ability to respond to any given situation. I choose my behavior; no one makes me do anything. I take ownership of my choices.

¤ Integrity: behaving in alignment with my highest values. I focus on doing my best. I don't play to win at all costs. How I play the game is more important than winning.

¤ Honesty: telling my truth—directly and respectfully. I don't hold back what I believe I need to say. Nor do I intentionally break down someone's self-esteem.

¤ Humility: being curious. A curious mindset acknowledges that my truth is just one point of view. I can't see the whole picture; I see things only through my eyes. Other points of view are equally valid.

These values are my North Star. They invisibly guide me, sitting below the surface, in the dark, like ninja warriors ready to do their job. They're in the back of my mind every day.

Tangible goals and process goals

When I play a tennis match, I have a tangible goal—I want to win the match. My process goal is to prepare for it and play my best, knowing full well I don't control the outcome. Having a process goal is my support underneath the tangible goal. I'm better prepared now to accept victory or defeat. If I win, I don't gloat; I'm just thankful for how I played. If I lose, I'm gracious in defeat and committed to getting better.

When you have a tangible goal and a process goal, you can strive for anything you want while having a built-in safety net to protect you from falling if you fail to achieve your process goal.

When it came to that job interview, I had a tangible goal, which was to get the job. Plus, I had a process goal, which was to prepare for the interview. But I was overly attached to the outcome, the tangible goal. I placed too much emphasis on it, and as a result, my performance was weak, and I suffered mentally and emotionally.

*   *   *

After the interview fiasco, I adjusted the way I approached my goals. I put more attention on how I work on my goals and less on the goal itself.

In early 2011, I interviewed for another sales job with a company based in Scotland. I certainly wanted the job but didn't have a meltdown this time. They hired me.

These days, I spend most of my time writing. Some days it goes well; some days, it's hard. No matter how it goes, my goal is to do my best—write from my heart, tell the truth, and have fun doing it.

For me, nothing beats living my life in alignment with my values because I know lasting peace of mind and fulfillment come from how I live.

Listening and Curiosity
Make a Better World

Not by being tougher or better than

Humans are fragile creatures even though some of us look confident and tough and can swagger around like we're going to punch anyone that gets in our way. Social media is often the perfect place to strut our stuff and promote our beliefs and opinions with the fiery enthusiasm of a stand-up preacher on the Santa Monica Pier or the street corners of New York City. Whether you asked for it or not, you're going to get an earful. It's easy to be tough, spouting beliefs and opinions. But it's usually not so easy to find our humanity when someone disagrees with us.

When we have a strong opinion, the first move is usually to defend and then attack. Defend our position. Fortify it. Bring in the sandbags. Get out the mortars and blow the enemy to bits with a seething I'm-going-to-make-you-pay-for-your-stupid-beliefs verbal barrage. Increase the volume and overwhelm them with more content supported by carefully selected data that backs up our position.

However, the wise person doesn't defend or attack. The wise person knows there is nothing to protect, no hill to die on, no castle to storm. There's no one to convince or persuade us because no one has the right to change someone else's mind. The most sacred of human freedoms is making our own choices, choosing our own attitude, and finding our own path.

Peace and resolution can never be achieved through coercion, separation, incentives, force, intimidation, bribery, or threats.

The wise person pauses first and carefully considers the situation before engagement. They ask themselves, "What is to be gained from having this conversation?" If they choose to engage in something, they inquire first. Then they listen. The wise person values knowledge and learning; they overlook "good" and being right. They might learn something new. They might be wrong. First and foremost, they are curious because they want to understand why someone thinks the way they do.

"What is to be gained from having this conversation?"

Wise people do this because they know that needing to be right is an unconscious game played by those who believe they can't possibly be wrong—ever. But arrogance usually brings down the seemingly invincible—those that place themselves above others intellectually, spiritually, physically, and socially.

Arrogance holds hands with greed—the insatiable desire to win the grand illusion that life is some race to see who can accumulate the most knowledge, the most friends, the most toys, the most wealth, the most fantastic rocket ship. The wise person knows their ego is fragile, and they know that identifying with the ego is a prime invitation to suffering. So instead, they identify with their heart and inner self. In that space, there is nothing to defend, no need to be right, no need to be afraid, nothing to prove to anyone. The only goal is to live in alignment with their highest values and help any situation move toward goodness.

Today will pass

When each day ends, the only thing left is our memories of what we did, what we said, and how we treated others. We'll be proud of ourselves or the hungry ghosts of guilt and remorse will haunt us. It's up to us, every moment. What path do we choose? We choose the simplest thing right now. Listening with an open mind and a curious heart seems to be one of the hardest things to do.

What's so hard or so threatening about listening to someone we disagree with?

It's hard—terribly hard—to listen to someone who has different beliefs from us when our heads are full of noise, emotion, anger, and righteousness and when we are mired in the staunch belief that we cannot possibly be wrong. When the poison fills us up, of course, we can't listen. We can't bear to take in anything that might threaten our *idea* of what the world should look like. We think if we have to give up our world, we give up ourselves and everything we stand for. We might have to face embarrassment. We might have to apologize and admit we didn't know everything. We wouldn't be so tough. We'd be fragile, vulnerable, open, frightened, looking for safety—realizing those around us are just like us.

But safety and equanimity do exist. We don't have to give up everything we believe, but we do have to drop the arrogance and find the part of us that aches for calm and peace—our higher self.

*   *   *

The higher self is where we find our true inner strength and humanity. And it's closer than we think. It's right inside of us, one breath away. The higher self is not a theory or some imaginary concept. Our higher self is our life force, giving us life, giving us hope. Those that tap into it find a source of peace unlike anything we can find in the world around us. And when we find peace with ourselves, we're more apt to pause, listen, and be curious. We realize the way to build a better world is by being wiser, not tougher.

Two Phrases That Drain Our Power

It's time to purge "I have to" and "I should" for good

I recently received an email from a friend explaining why he wasn't going to sign up for my newsletter.

"I'm deluged with stuff I have to read, so unfortunately I will need to decline your offer," he said.

While it was thoughtful of him to let me know he didn't want to sign up for my newsletter, I was more interested in his use of the phrase "have to." When someone says, "I have to," alarm bells go off in my head. I start wondering what's going on under the surface. "I have to" is a linguistic shortcut that diminishes personal choice and responsibility. In other words, no one is making my friend read anything; he can *choose* to read it—just like he chooses what to eat every day.

His response reminded me how difficult it can be for us to express ourselves honestly and respectfully sometimes. He could have said, "Thanks for asking me to join your mailing list. I'm saying No because I'm cutting back on all incoming email." Or "Thanks for asking, but No. I've got other priorities I want to focus on right now." Or "I'm deluged with stuff I want to read, and as much as I'd like to, I don't want to take on any more." I could easily accept any of those responses at face value.

The problem with "have to"

"I have to . . ." is often used as a smokescreen for the real truth, hidden in service of being socially polite or politically correct. The expression is supposed to make things easier for us to accept, but if we pay attention, we'll notice there's often more to the story—something has been left out or sanitized.

"I have to" and "I should" are close relatives and co-conspirators. "I should call my parents." "I have to be more serious about getting

79

up earlier." "I should learn to meditate." "I have to stop eating so much dessert." By repeatedly using these expressions, we create a guilt-ridden, inauthentic mindset and conveniently create distance between ourselves and reality.

Saying, "I should call my parents" means you aren't calling them and yet believe there is a reason to do so. Telling yourself you should call them is a pleasant way to acknowledge your good intentions. You're temporarily off the hook and feel better about yourself, except you haven't committed to doing anything or clarifying what you want to do. Maybe you're busy or not in the right frame of mind. Perhaps you don't want to call them at all. Fine. Get in touch with what you want. Be honest with yourself, whatever the truth is.

Reclaim your power

We slowly give away our power when we don't take responsibility for what we want to do. No one is forcing us to do anything, but how often do people stay in meetings, wanting to leave, but continue to sit there? Why not say, "Time for me to go. I have another commitment I want to keep"? Get up and leave. Saying "I want to" embraces the spirit of personal choice and responsibility—it's a statement of personal desire. On the other hand, "I have to" implies obligation, duty, and requirement. They are two very different attitudes.

But saying "I want to" comes with a price—being fully honest with yourself first and then figuring out how to speak truthfully and respectfully.

Taking responsibility for what we do in life begins with evaluating how we think because the way we think drives our language and behavior. Change your thinking, change your life. How we think defines who we are on the inside and create our self-image. Likewise, what we say or do defines us on the outside and builds our reputation in the world. When we pay more attention to our inner dialogue, we'll discover who's running the show, and in some cases, it's not the real us; it's an impostor who has taken control.

The impostor

The impostor wants to be liked, do the right thing, look good, and avoid rocking the boat. The impostor is our ego, our talkative mind, and has little interest in the truth because living the truth erases the role the impostor plays. The impostor won't say, "No. I don't want to go out with you anymore." Instead, the impostor will ghost people and hide in its deluded inner world, convincing us we're decent, honest human beings. But, when we behave without regard for others and lie to ourselves, we're under the spell of the impostor. Little things in life quickly become big things.

By saying "I have to" repeatedly, we also create a habit. After a while, you don't notice it's become part of your everyday language—you're on autopilot. Imagine you're out with someone on a first date, it's not going well, and you want the miserable evening to end. You could say, "I have to get going now. I'll be in touch." Guess what? Everyone can smell that bullshit a mile away. So how about saying, "Hey, look. To be honest, I'm not feeling the connection I'm looking for, so I'd like to call it a night." Wouldn't you respect someone more if they were honest and polite, and wouldn't you feel better about yourself if *you* were?

You can break the spell of the impostor

The next time you're about to say, "I have to," "I should," or "I need to," try saying, "I want to," "I choose to," "I have other priorities right now," or "No, I don't want to do that." When you're honest and respectful, you feel empowered, and you'll set an example for others, too.

*   *   *

And the best news? You will leave none of us guessing what you mean when you say what you want. You'll be crystal clear.

All Personal Growth Starts
with an Ending

The three phases of personal change

Going through a significant personal change like a relationship break-up or the loss of a loved one is difficult mentally, physically, and emotionally. It's easy to experience shock, anger, resentment, and grieving for weeks or months at a time. As much as we'd like to move on, we find ourselves seemingly stuck in a Groundhog Day type of funk. We wonder what's wrong with us.

But nothing is wrong. We're going through stages of transition, and there's no skipping any of them. William Bridges, author of *Transitions: Making Sense of Life's Changes,* explains that while change is external—moving from one city to another, for example—transition or adaptation to change is an internal, psychological process.

Bridges says there are three phases to transitioning—endings, neutral zone, and new beginnings. *Endings* occur when there are significant changes in relationships, employment, home life, finances, lifestyle, and inner being. The *neutral zone* is a place of emptiness, a kind of no man's land where endings are not resolved, and the future is not clear. *New beginnings* are characterized by embracing new possibilities, acceptance, and adapting willingly.

If you're in the endings phase, you might feel sad, angry, or fearful. If you are in the neutral zone, you might experience uncertainty, confusion, or disorientation. If you're in the new beginning phase, you likely feel enthusiastic, energetic, and optimistic.

Welcome to the neutral zone

The neutral zone, on the other hand, is like a twilight zone—neither completely dark nor fully light. It's gray and foggy, and we can't see clearly. Part of us is still in the ending phase—holding on to what has been familiar—while we suffer and resist. Another part has a foot in the new beginning, trying to adjust to a new world. We sense the future, but it's just beyond our reach. So, we find ourselves somewhere in the middle, feeling disoriented. But we can't just skip the neutral zone and jump right into the new beginning. We have to wander through it, getting flashes of the past and how things used to be.

Emotions and memories are stirred up. We feel unsettled and angry at the whole damn thing. Our psyche needs time to process, to grieve, and to let go. It doesn't happen overnight.

In the neutral zone, we're not sure who to believe or trust. We might feel confused, not entirely on our game, but we carry on. We can't quite put our finger on why things aren't getting better faster. Something has happened that we didn't initiate, and now we're figuring out how to deal with it. We haven't been here before—not like this. We're flying without radar, and we don't feel like ourselves.

This notion of the phases of personal growth has deep roots in human history. Arnold van Gennep, a Dutch/French anthropologist who studied people, culture, and their habits and customs, wrote about the phases of transitions in *The Rites of Passage*, published in 1909. Van Gennep's research significantly influenced Joseph Campbell's *The Hero with a Thousand Faces*, which George Lucas subsequently studied and integrated into his Hollywood movies. The hero's journey is easy to spot on the big screen, but it's not easy to recognize when it's happening to us. We dig in our heels, hunker down, resist, and forget that all personal growth starts with an ending.

We don't have the same understanding of transitions in our modern world as ancient cultures had. In many tribal cultures, elders took young people away from the community for a rite of passage to help them transition into adulthood.

On the other hand, the rites of passage of today—high school graduations, bar mitzvahs or bat mitzvahs, retirement celebrations, and others—have mostly been reduced to events and parties. We're more focused on external events and less on our internal psychological processes. The discussion around the deeper meaning of these life events has been lost.

Instead of elders having a meaningful role in modern society, we have our peer groups. When we are in the neutral zone, internally fragmented, we look for validation of our experiences. We look for safety and security and those who think like us and are experiencing what we are.

Perhaps this explains the exceptional polarization occurring in our culture now. We want to be with like-minded people who can align with our view of reality during a time of significant disorientation.

A time of renewal

The good news, according to Bridges, is that the neutral zone is also a time of renewal and the birthplace of the future. His wife and business partner, Susan Bridges, writes, "The essence of life takes place in the neutral zone phase of transition. It is in that interim spaciousness that all possibilities, creativity, and innovative ideas can come to life and flourish."

Here is a summary of each phase of Bridges' model and the typical emotions associated with them:

Endings	Neutral Zone	New Beginnings
Angry	Confused	Excited
Shocked	Depressed	Energized
In Denial	Apathetic	Enthusiastic
Fearful	Lethargic	Positive
Sad	Disoriented	Happy
	Adapted by the author from the work of William Bridges	

If you're in the endings phase or the neutral zone, here are some actions that might help you move to new beginnings:

¤ Focus on what is in your control—your attitude and the way you show up. Remain hopeful and optimistic.

¤ If you like to talk things out, find someone you trust who can listen. If you don't like to talk, grab a pen and write. Writing on paper is a powerful way to release and process emotions—more than typing on a computer.

¤ Become clear about what you want in new beginnings. Figure out what you can do and do it. The smallest steps forward make a big difference.

¤ Be clear about what is ending, if anything, for you. Discuss it; acknowledge it. Mark the ending by having a ceremony.

¤ Exercise and move your body regularly. The body stores stress and trauma; movement helps release it.

¤ Make a list of what you can stop, start, or continue.

¤ Take time for yourself. Do something you love every day. Be kind to yourself.

¤ Be creative. Make something, bake something, build something, paint something. It helps to unleash positive energy, which helps the healing process.

¤ Celebrate small victories and keep track of your progress toward your goals.

¤ Stand tall. Be proud of who you are and all you have accomplished in your life.

* * *

It's time to plant the seeds of what you want in life. Nurture those seeds and yourself. New beginnings are coming.

Lessons from Black Holes

The answers are in the darkness

A black hole is a place in space where a tremendous amount of matter is packed into a very tiny area. Think of a star 10 times larger than the sun squeezed into the size of a city like Boston. Its gravity is so strong that light doesn't escape. Black holes are hard to detect, but scientists locate them through their influence on surrounding stars. They have great power over anything that comes near them, and, despite their name, they contain plenty of light.

When we find ourselves in darkness, we become vulnerable to fear—fear for our safety, fear of an uncertain future, fear of living in an out-of-control world, and fear of a life without purpose, meaning, or happiness. Fear robs us of being present. It distracts us from reality. We start to feel empty, and we look for ways to fill ourselves.

Who didn't say "I can't wait for the pandemic to be over?" Who didn't need to come to terms with the reality that things were going to take longer than we had hoped. It was depressing—it felt like we were in a black hole—trying to escape but unable to do so. We worried we might take on the qualities of that black hole, absorbing the chaos around us and collapsing into ourselves, losing ourselves in the darkness, and forgetting who we are.

We looked around for reassurance. Who could we trust? Who could we bet on to bring us to safety? We desperately wanted to believe in goodness. We looked around to fill the yearning within and want the future to be better. We waited for it, hoped for it. We unconsciously looked through the present moment, hungry for what we wanted: a stable life that's rich with meaning and peace.

Sure, if we're locked down, we want more freedom. We want to see our friends again; we want everyone to get the vaccine. We want

to stay healthy. We want our previous job back or a better job for the
future. We want to see our friends in person and to be mask-free.
But if we spent too much time wanting the future to be as we imagine, we miss living in the present, and we missed the opportunity to
be at peace.

We *don't* want to be an empty black hole, attaching ourselves to
everything around us. We want to be full. But how do we do it?

After a lifetime of practicing meditation, I've found that when we
realize the source of satisfaction is within us and when we find a way
to connect to it, our quality of life improves. We start living from the
inside out, not the outside in. It's not a slogan from positive psychology. "The source of happiness is within." It's real, but we must look
through the darkness deep inside ourselves to find it.

Living in the here and now is the key to greater peace of mind

The past is gone, there is no future, and there is no fear. When we give
up waiting for the future, we realize the present moment is perfect
and has everything we need. The space within us that wants more is
filled. This is where peace is—in the present. The past is gone; there
is no future, and there is no fear.

Every day, I ask myself: *Where* will I focus my energy? I can't
change most things around me, but what I do with my time and attention is mine. I get to choose how I show up and who I will be on any
given day. I opt to face my fears or bury them through distraction. I
decide if I'll be a black hole, sucking the life out of myself and those
around me, or if I'll be someone who shines brightly.

When we live from the inside out, we can more easily find
our true selves. We're less consumed with continually plugging
ourselves into the world. We let ourselves take time to reflect and
recharge—and as a result, we're less distracted. We can more easily
see our fears, large or small. Fear doesn't come from being in the
light; it comes from being in the dark. Ask yourself, "What am I

afraid of?" Write everything down. I bet you'll find one common thread: the future.

Worrying about the future takes you out of being in the present, which is the only place where you can do anything about what you fear. Fear of the future is a convenient anaesthetic from the Big Fear. The Big Fear, which comes from forgetting who you are, is the fear of wasting your life. The good news is that when you start asking questions like "What is my purpose?" "What is my calling?" and "Who is my true self?" you're on the doorstep of transformation.

As my spiritual practice has grown over the years, I've noticed that my fear of a wasted life is directly related to losing touch with my higher self. The greater the disconnection from my higher self, the more I worry. The greater connection, the less I worry. When I drift away from my inner self, I try to find myself in all the wrong places. So, I scramble, grabbing at things that look like they might be the answer—but they're not, and I know it.

Going into the darkness

Here is a practice I do every day. Consider it a brief introduction to a much larger topic and only one of the many ways to enter your inner world.

Find a quiet space for 10 minutes. Get comfortable. Take a few deep, long breaths, and close your eyes. Move your awareness to your breath, following it as your lungs expand and contract slowly. Enjoy the darkness. It appears to be dark, but it's not. Within the darkness, it's milky, like a galaxy of stars. Don't look past it. Look at it and allow your gaze to be absorbed. Continue to breathe slowly and deeply. There's nothing to try to do or to find. Just be. Let go of any expectations and thoughts that wander in. Open yourself to receive what is there. Let whatever happens come to you. There is no need to do anything. If you experience something, be thankful. If you don't, be thankful. Be patient and continue practicing regularly.

*   *   *

When we lose something, we often find it where we least expect it. Black holes might seem like the last place in the universe to find light, but it's there. The same holds true for us. In the least likely place within us, where it seems dark and empty, we find our true selves, full of light and contentment.

PART 3

Building Meaningful Relationships

Wisdom Begins When You Ask
This One Question

Create a better world through curiosity, not judgment

A friend of mine recently posted a picture on Facebook mocking people that had different beliefs than his. I was disappointed but not surprised. It happens when we believe we are right and we have to make those who differ from us wrong in order to support our position. Doing this kind of thing is easier to do when we share our beliefs with a large group because we've got the majority standing with us; there's power in numbers. Groupthink.

It's easy to criticize others when we feel there's little risk of retaliation. Social bullying is wrong, harmful, and divisive. But perpetrators feel justified because they believe their point of view is the only possible view. They want to promote their beliefs at any cost, even if it means labeling, criticizing, and judging others.

This social phenomenon is not dissimilar to the influence of the Catholic Church in medieval times. During that age of intellectual darkness, religious dogma dictated how people should think and behave. Anyone disagreeing with this way of thinking was labeled a heretic and either rehabilitated, persecuted, or killed. The Salem witch trials in 1692 were another example of the fear of the unknown, fueled by mass hysteria, leading to the persecution and death of innocent men and women.

We need a more tolerant, inclusive world

These may seem like extreme examples, but they all share a common root system: the compulsion to impose opinions on others and punish them for not getting in line with the accepted narrative. We don't need more of this right now. We need less—much less—because we're living in unprecedented, highly stressful times. In fact, the compulsion to impose opinions on others needs to stop. If we want to get through life safely, we need to build a better, kinder, more inclusive world.

When we're ridiculed or persecuted for how we look, think, or behave, we go silent or dig in more and resist. Either way, the chance for open and honest dialogue decreases as people further solidify their positions, while the gap between them grows wider and deeper. The bigger the gap, the easier it is to argue. But nobody wins an argument; there are only losers.

The power of curiosity

The way to close the gap is to be courageous enough to ask, "What don't I know?" It takes courage because you must make yourself vulnerable. You have to admit you don't know everything. You risk looking good by seeking the truth because you might find out you're wrong or don't know as much as you initially thought you did. You might have to acknowledge that those you persecuted for their beliefs knew something you didn't. You might even have to apologize, God forbid.

It's humbling and possibly hurtful when you realize you were wrong. Nonetheless, you'll find that it's worth it in the long run. Asking ourselves, "What don't I know?" replaces arrogance with curiosity, judgment with openness, division with connection, and argument with dialogue. Life is not about being right. It's about learning, growth, and finding your way to the truth.

A few years ago, I started using this "What don't I know?" question when my boss asked me to build a relationship with a guy who managed a business in another division of the company. She said, "Get to know him. Get curious." I had my doubts because when I first met him at a social event, I found him loud and brash—not particularly my kind of guy. I wondered how I'd overcome my first impression and find a way to build a decent relationship with him.

We set up an introductory phone meeting, and when we started the call, I said, "Why don't we start by talking about what we don't know about each other?" He agreed, and we shared our professional and personal backgrounds, coloring in the details with stories about various wins and losses. The more we talked, the more we discovered how much we had in common, and I got a glimpse into his larger-than-life personality. I could finally see how he was wired and what made him tick. An hour later, I hung up the phone, thinking, "I can work with this guy." We collaborated for the next few years and have since remained good friends.

It all started with just a tiny bit of curiosity.

Getting back to my friend on Facebook: He didn't care if he offended me or anyone else. I believe everyone has the right to express their opinions and stand up for what they believe. However, expressing an opinion about the wrongness of a differing point of view merely creates more disagreement and friction. Our fractured world doesn't need more division. We need more healing and tolerance of differences—and the desire to understand why someone maintains those different thoughts.

*　　*　　*

Before you make a judgment about someone, act on incomplete information, or assume everyone thinks like you, ask yourself, "What don't I know about this situation, behavior, or person?" Chances are, you'll find something valuable, and you'll be glad you took the time to ask. Plus, you'll help make the world just a tiny bit better.

Four Steps to Being Honest.
Even When It's Hard.

A guide to saying the quiet part loud

Have you ever struggled with saying what's really on your mind? We all do. When we're not being fully honest with others, it's often because:

¤ We don't want to be rejected

¤ We don't want to upset the other person or damage our relationship with them

¤ We don't want the conversation to get out of control

¤ We don't know how to raise a difficult issue skillfully.

In her book, *Fierce Conversations,* Susan Scott wrote: "Never be afraid of the conversations you're having. Be afraid of the conversations you're not having."

But when we don't speak honestly, problems can occur. For example, unexpressed thoughts and feelings can get bottled up and come pouring out in angry outbursts like "You always do that!" or "You never clean up after yourself!" You suffer by not saying what you think and feel, and angry outbursts create unnecessary conflict.

Another problem is that people can often sense when someone isn't saying what they really think and feel. They wonder what's going on. And, if you're working on a team and holding back what you think are good ideas only because they run counter to the groupthink, you may be unintentionally holding back the team's success.

Four strategies to start honest conversations

The hardest part of speaking honestly is often the entry point—what to say and how to say it. A conversation is likely to go better if it starts well. Here are four strategies that can help you begin those honest conversations.

1. Recognize when you aren't saying what you are thinking or feeling.

Our human brains process information faster than we talk. We think even when we are listening. Most of us have relatively good filters, so we monitor and manage a stream of thoughts and feelings during a conversation. But there's a problem when we say one thing but think and feel something entirely different. There's a problem when we say "Great! I look forward to speaking with you again soon!" while our inside voice is saying "I have no interest at all in speaking with them—ever."

When you don't say what you think and feel, you leave the most critical part of you out of the conversation—and you know it. You're suppressing what's known as the "left-hand column."

Chris Argyris and Donald Schon, former professors at Harvard and MIT, respectively, created a tool called the "left-hand column framework," which was designed to improve communication effectiveness. In his classes, Argyris asked students to take a piece of paper and draw a line down the middle. In the left-hand column, they jotted down what they were thinking during a conversation but did not say out loud. In the right-hand column, they wrote what each person actually said. In most cases, the two columns looked quite different.

In a difficult conversation, our left-hand column is often full of toxic thoughts, feelings, judgments, accusations, assumptions, and criticisms. We don't ask for "left-hand column" thoughts; they're usually a reaction to something upsetting. These unspoken thoughts rise to the surface like bubbles in a glass of champagne.

With an unmanaged left-hand column, you might:

¤ Say Yes to things you don't want to do or say you're okay with something you're not.

¤ Bottle up your feelings and grow resentful.

¤ Send mixed messages by saying one thing but thinking
  another.

Besides causing internal problems for you, suppressing your left-
hand column can cause other problems, too:

¤ Everyone knows when someone is not being entirely truthful with them. They pick up on the tone of voice and body
  language. When you have a left-hand column, people
  sense it.

¤ We know that blurting out our left-hand column in its raw,
  toxic form is unacceptable. We'll feel bad about saying
  something rude, and we will likely damage the relationship. But if we keep that left-hand column bottled up long
  enough, we might eventually say something we regret.

So, we have a four-pronged dilemma—a quadrilemma. Your
left-hand column is often toxic. You're damned if you say it, you're
damned if you don't say it, and others have a sense of what you are
thinking anyway.

It's hard to speak honestly and respectfully if you don't clean it up.

2. Detoxify what you are thinking or feeling.

A "left-hand column" shows up because something you care about
is at risk. You can detoxify the it by uncovering your essential truth
and saying it honestly and respectfully. Ask yourself:

¤ What do I care about that's at risk?

¤ What's bothering me?

Here's an example. It's important to me to be on time for meetings;
I value my own and other people's time. So, if someone is repeatedly
late for an appointment, I become irritated, and my left-hand column
gets loaded up with things like, "They're late again. What's wrong
with them? Idiot. Don't they have any concern for others?"

When I answered the questions above, I discovered I felt disrespected because when someone shows up late a lot and doesn't let me know ahead of time, I consider them inconsiderate of me and my time. Here's how I could communicate this honestly and respectfully:

"I have a concern. We've discussed the importance of punctuality before; we're both busy. We agreed to meet at 3:00 p.m., but you arrived at 3:15 and didn't let me know you were running late. I feel disrespected. I know it's not your intention to do so. Tell me what happened?"

Just because I do this doesn't mean the problem is solved. I've still got to deal with the response. But at least I didn't suppress my irritation. I brought it up honestly and respectfully, which is the most important thing. The key points here are:

- The kind of thoughts we put in a left-hand column are full of valuable information and contain our essential truth. They need to be detoxified to be helpful.

- We can detoxify our "left-hand column" by recognizing what it is that we care about that's at risk.

- We can still express ourselves honestly and respectfully. Use phrases like "I have a concern ..." "My experience is ..." or "My opinion is ..." to open up a conversation.

3. Have a learning mindset

A learning mindset is open and curious. For this reason, those with a learning mindset are open to the ideas and perspectives of others. They realize they might have different subjective experiences. They respect and value others' opinions.

On the other hand, when we have a closed mindset, we believe our view of the world is the only possible reality. A closed mindset renders us closed to others' ideas. We seek to look good at all costs and want to prove others wrong.

When you have a learning mindset, it becomes much easier to speak honestly. When you're talking with someone, make it your intention to share about yourself, inform them about events, or create a pleasant dialog in the moment. Avoid trying to convince someone that your point of view is the right one. You don't have to have everything figured out before speaking. You have the right to offer an opinion, make a suggestion, or propose a potential solution.

Here are three ways to speak with a learning mindset:

¤ When you're sharing your thoughts and opinions about something—beyond the facts of the matter—be sure to point out you're sharing your personal views. For example, say, "In my view . . ." or "The way that I see this is . . ."

¤ Share your views (even if they're incomplete) and remain open to challenges from others: "I am thinking out loud here . . ." "I haven't figured this out completely yet . . ."

¤ Listen to others' thoughts and opinions and genuinely try to understand why they think, act, or feel like they do. "I am curious to understand why . . ." "Why do you say that?"

When you have a learning mindset, it's easier to be honest because you're simply sharing your experiences or opinions.

4. Use the Kitchen Conversation Technique

Imagine for a moment that I've invited you to dinner at my home at 7:00 p.m. this Saturday. You show up just as I'm putting everything out on the dining room table. We enjoy a brief cocktail, and then we eat. You love the cauliflower chickpea curry with lemon basmati rice and zucchini flatbread I made and ask, "How did you do that?"

I smile and say, "Ah, so you would like to have a *kitchen* conversation." You nod your head. So, I say, "Well then, come next week at 5:00 p.m. We'll spend some time in the kitchen first, and I'll show you how I make everything."

A *dining room* conversation is like presenting a fully cooked dinner. A *kitchen* conversation shows and explains how the dinner was cooked.

A kitchen conversation explains a lot. You pull back the curtain and define the facts, data, and rationale as you see them. You explain your logic and reasoning. You do this not to prove you are right but to nurture dialogue and encourage others to reach their own conclusions.

Conversations and relationships break down when people don't disclose the reasoning behind an idea, proposal, critique, or suggestion. It's one thing to tell someone the project they're working on wouldn't work (dining room conversation). It's another thing to explain why you think so (kitchen conversation).

And the process goes both ways. When someone states their opinion without backing it up with facts or reasoning, inquiring about how they arrived at their conclusion asks for a kitchen conversation. It demonstrates your openness and willingness to learn and understand another perspective.

Here are some other ways you can use the Kitchen Conversation Technique:

- ¤ If someone doesn't explain their reasoning, politely say, "I understand you believe 'ABC' is the correct way to proceed on the project. Help me understand why you think that way?"

- ¤ When you have an idea you want to bring up but aren't sure how to do it, say, "Look, I have an idea here. I think it's got potential, and here's why. I want to bring it up for discussion."

A kitchen conversation makes speaking honestly easier because you explain your thought process, your interpretation of the facts, and your point of view. You share not just what you think but why you think the way you do. The next time you hesitate to speak honestly, remember these four strategies:

- ¤ Recognize when you have a left-hand column.
- ¤ Detoxify it by asking yourself what you feel might be at risk.
- ¤ Tap into a learning mindset.
- ¤ Have a kitchen conversation.

There are times, of course, when it's best to say nothing. And there are times when speaking honestly is the right thing to do.

Avoid Stupid Arguments
with Verbal Aikido

The martial art of talking with someone
who disagrees with you

W ords have power. Once we put them out there, we can't take them back. Expressions like "I didn't mean to say that" or "I was only kidding" come too late. So, why do couples get into needless arguments? Jeffery S. Smith, MD, writes in *Psychology Today*: "The cause of argument and fights is a lack of mutual, empathic understanding. When empathy is not engaged, then people revert to a self-protective mode and become judgmental. The result is a bad feeling on both sides and no happy ending. People want to be understood, not just heard."

Author Daniel Kahneman's theory of two different systems of thinking, what he calls "System 1" and "System 2," sheds light on why we sometimes lose the ability to be empathetic in our relationships.

System 1 thinking operates quickly and without concentrated effort, Kahneman says. It's more unconscious, irrational, and emotional. We use it when we're driving a car on an empty road, reading words on a giant billboard, doing something familiar, or something that looks easy, like a simple math problem.

System 2, on the other hand, involves effort and attention. It's logical, rational, and conscious. We use it when solving complicated calculations, when adjusting our behavior in a social situation, or when searching for a specific person in a crowd.

If something looks easy, we use System 1, the more unconscious method of thinking. But if we use System 1 alone, we're more likely to make assumptions, jump to conclusions and not listen attentively. This might explain one of the challenges of being in a relationship: We get used to our partner's thought patterns and behavior, they become familiar and almost predictable, and we go on autopilot and default to System 1. Especially when we get triggered, frustrated, or stressed. It's easy to get emotional and defensive. Empathy can be elusive.

Three strategies to access empathy and avoid unnecessary arguments

1. Speak with humility

While a lack of empathy may be the underlying cause of arguments, the words we use are the delivery system. The way we express ourselves and our opinions either invites dialogue or shuts it down. Let's talk about opinions for a moment.

Opinions are subjective and, when expressed in the first person— speaking about "I"— are generally constructive. They invite differing viewpoints and lay the foundation for resolving conflict. In contrast, using language in the second or third person—talking about "you" or "them"—closes out dialogue and invites defensiveness. An opinion presented as a fact can be toxic and can become a surefire way to make someone defensive.

Here are some examples of expressing toxic opinions:

"You're wrong."

"That's stupid."

"You aren't thinking clearly."

"You shouldn't have done that."

"You always do that."

Contrast expressing those opinions with these:

"I don't understand."

"I disagree."

"I feel annoyed."

"I prefer something different."

"I have a concern."

These "I" statements are examples of first-person communication and of owning your opinion, a critical element of humility—and, therefore, empathy. Speaking with humility will cool a conversation that's getting too hot. It only takes one conscious person to stop an argument.

2. Actively listen

Be present: We've all experienced the disappointment of speaking to someone who is clearly busy or distracted but says, "Go ahead, I'm listening." It feels disrespectful and can derail a conversation quickly. Be fully attentive and look at the person you are speaking to.

Be quiet: If you are aware that you interrupt people, stop doing it. It conveys that you are more interested in getting your point across than anything else. Once you do sense that you interrupt, it's a good sign that you aren't listening.

Demonstrate your presence: If you sit silently like a statue, no one knows whether you're actually listening. Nodding gently or saying "Mm-hmm" or "Uh-huh" will help encourage the other person to explain themselves fully. Silent attention only makes people wonder if anyone is home.

Get curious: Questions show interest and help the other person feel valued. In *The 7 Habits of Highly Effective People*, Stephen Covey writes, "Seek first to understand, then to be understood." When something doesn't make sense to you or you start to feel agitated, ask yourself: *What don't I know? Is there something I am missing? What am I curious about?*

Use reflective listening: Summarize what you think you have heard and check to make sure you have it right. "Here's what I hear you saying and what is important to you… Is this correct?" If you don't have it right, you can try again. You aren't agreeing—you are just demon-strating you understand.

If you don't understand, say "I don't understand or "Help me out. I'm not getting it." It's counterproductive to say "You are not making sense." This creates more defensiveness and blames the other person.

3. Verbal Aikido

Aikido is a modern Japanese martial art that uses the principles of nonresistance to neutralize an opponent. Translated to English, the term means "the way of harmonious spirit." Aikido does not offer aggressive or defensive maneuvers but instead uses the energy of an opponent to divert and redirect an attack harmlessly. The philoso-phy is based on peaceful resolution and self-improvement.

Arguments are like two people physically pushing each other. One pushes, the other pushes back, then the other pushes back harder. Nothing is accomplished, and everybody feels bad. Verbal Aikido can defuse conflicts and can help both individuals rekindle empathy.

Let's say my wife and I are arguing. She says "That's a dumb idea; it won't work." If I say "You're wrong," I'm just pushing back on her, creating more friction. If I agree with her but don't mean it, I'm not being truthful, and I'll wind up being resentful. Verbal Aikido, however, can help stop the "pushing."

These are the steps to practicing verbal Aikido:

Yield. I can defuse the situation by acknowledging her point of view and reframing it slightly to help her recognize and own her opin-ion. I avoid saying anything aggressive or defensive, but I might say "You think it's a dumb idea," which helps her take ownership of the opinion she presented as a fact. That's the first step in redirecting the verbal attack.

Inquire. Assuming she says "Yes, I do think it's a dumb idea," I can say "Okay, help me understand why you think it's dumb." I want to invite her to share not just what she thinks but why she thinks that way. I'm curious to understand her thinking and perspective.

Share. Then, I explain why I think the way I do. "I think it's a good idea because . . ." This creates balance in the conversation and opens up a discussion, not just about our opinions, but about what is behind them. Arguments are solved through dialogue.

Resolve. As we talk more, if she offers convincing ideas, I can change my mind. If I still don't agree, I can say "Let's find a solution that works for both of us." We may compromise and move ahead together, or we may agree to disagree, but at least we understand why we think the way we do, and that is a better outcome than arguing.

*   *   *

Arguments are inevitable in relationships, but by being mindful and skillful, we can speak wisely, listen actively, and bring empathy and love into our conversations—even the tough ones.

How to Be a More
Interesting Conversationalist

Four simple steps for better communication

Mark Goulston, author of *Just Listen*, wrote that people typically shut down after listening to someone talk for more than 40 seconds. And I recently had a first-hand experience of it.

My houseguest, someone I didn't know very well, turned out to be quite the talker. As we sat together after dinner, his verbal stream of consciousness washed over me, and I wondered when he might pause to take a breath. He didn't.

I felt myself shutting down, losing interest, not just in listening to him but also in saying anything. The nonstop talking continued at breakfast the next morning and into the afternoon activities. Not one question did he ask of me. Not surprisingly, I didn't feel any meaningful connection with him when we said our goodbyes later that day.

I had quite a different experience a month earlier when a business acquaintance introduced me to someone she thought I might get along with. He and I had an hour-long Zoom call, a delightful exchange about our personal and professional lives. We learned about each other—he asked great questions, listened without interrupting, and I did the same. The hour flew by, and we agreed to have another call. I hung up the phone, thinking, *"Great guy. Be happy to chat with him again."* We made a good connection and created a warm friendship.

When people talk too much, you only get to know the part of themselves they're speaking about, and that might or might not interest you. They certainly don't get to know you. As a result, no meaningful bond is formed, so why would you look forward to another interaction?

Talking too much is not attractive or socially polite. At its worst, it can be rude, narcissistic, and damaging to your credibility.

From my experience as a leadership consultant and executive coach, here are four principles that can help you be a more interesting conversationalist in your business and personal life.

1. Manage your internal noise

Listening takes work because it's an active skill, not a passive one. I'll never forget the guy who kept looking over my shoulder at the people behind me as we were talking—it made me feel like he was somewhere else during the entire conversation. Our own overactive minds can create interference and get in our way. If you know you're distracted going into a conversation, say something like, "Please forgive me; I've got a lot on my mind. If you see me losing focus, it's not you."

Another common interference is mentally rehearsing what you will say when someone is speaking. It's not necessary, and it gets in the way of being fully present. Instead, just listen and put your attention totally on the other person.

When we manage our internal noise, we can be more present, which means we can catch the nuances of someone's tone of voice, facial expression, body language, and even what's not said. As a result, we can more easily reflect back what we heard through paraphrasing, clarifying, confirming, and asking meaningful follow-up questions. See my discussion of reflective listening in the previous essay.

2. Listen, acknowledge, and inquire

Charles Green, the author of *The Trusted Advisor*, says, "Listening is not a means to an end but is an end in itself." He points out that listening is not just a necessary task to be completed that earns you the right to speak. Instead, real listening creates a meaningful connection—it is an active process that signals genuine interest in the other person. When someone shows interest in us, we feel it, like it, and we're more apt to like and remember the person who listened to us.

Express interest in your partner's viewpoint. A conversation should be like a ball that gets passed back and forth between two people: one person speaks, tossing the ball, the other catches it—acknowledging the point being made, asking a question, or providing their point of view—and tosses it back. Catching the ball without any form of acknowledgment can leave the other person wondering if you're actually listening.

Even a small gesture like a head nod or simply saying "I see," or "Uh-huh" can demonstrate you're paying attention. Asking follow-up questions like 'Tell me more," or, "I'm intrigued when you said . . ." helps signal interest. Building on the last thing someone said is a great way to advance the conversation and demonstrate your engagement.

If you want someone to speak more, ask open-ended questions using questions that begin with "what," "how," or "why." On the other hand, if you want to limit someone's answers or get specific details, ask close-ended questions that can be answered with one word or short answers. For example, "Do you like red wine?" or "Do you want to go for a walk?"

3. Speak honestly and respectfully

Research from the Harvard University Social Cognitive and Affective Neuroscience (SCAN) lab found that when people talk about themselves, they activate the mesolimbic dopamine system in the brain, which is generally associated with reward and has been linked to the pleasurable feelings and motivational states associated with stimuli such as sex, cocaine, and good food. No wonder we like to talk about ourselves. But there's speaking about ourselves, and there's speaking with consideration for the other person.

We are naturally attracted to people who are authentic and truthful. We like straight talk. We also appreciate being respected by others. Conversations are more effective when both elements exist together—connection improves, and defensiveness decreases. Problems occur when honesty becomes brutal, demeaning, and hurtful. On the other hand, being respectful without honesty can show up as overly nice, insincere, and passive. When honesty and respect are integrated, we can be powerful and graceful—creating authenticity and effectiveness.

Leading by example is also key. Remember that you can set the tone for the conversation. If you want to add a personal touch to a conversation, use someone's name occasionally. It conveys warmth and caring. If you want the conversation to be more intimate, take the lead and share something appropriate in the context of the conversation. If you want someone to speak freely, ask for their advice. It's a powerful way to create a deeper connection.

Give permission to interrupt. If you know you tend to wander off-topic, let your conversation partner know up front and give them permission to interrupt or get you back on track. For example, "I'm a bit of a talker. If I go on too much, interrupt me." Self-disclosure is powerful and helps create more trust and openness.

4. Resolve differences

Conversations often break down because people want to look good and be right. It's a defense mechanism based on fear and self-protection. But even a contentious disagreement can be resolved if you look for underlying interests.

For example, a couple wants to go on vacation. One person wants to go hiking, the other to the beach. They each have their position, but if they ask each other "Why is that important to you?" they'll find underlying interests that open up possibilities to solve the problem.

"Why is hiking important to me? I like fresh air, exercise, and being in nature."

"Why is the beach important to me? I like to relax, feel the warmth of the sun, and swim in the water."

Both people want to be in nature, get fresh air, relax, and exercise; they have shared interests. They can brainstorm together to discover alternatives that satisfy their shared interests.

Another way to create transparent dialogue, surface inferences, and avoid potential problems is to use the phrase, "The story I'm telling myself is …" For example, "The story I'm telling myself when I don't hear from you for weeks at a time is you just don't care about our friendship as much as you did before." The other person might surprise you with something like: "No. I'm so sorry. I've had a rough few months dealing with family drama. It's been overwhelming."

If you feel yourself getting angry or agitated, remember to take a deep breath and ask a clarifying question before losing your cool and regretting it later. "Hey, I'm really not getting what you're saying. Please, start from the beginning and explain it again."

Don't get furious; get curious.

*   *   *

We spend a lot of our life in conversation. When we manage internal distractions, balance speaking with listening, and are ready to resolve any differences, we can become better conversationalists and develop stronger connections with our conversation partners. Elizabeth Lesser, author of *Cassandra Speaks* and other books, sums it up really well: "Don't persuade, defend, or interrupt. Be curious, be conversational, be real, and don't interrupt."

Opinions Are Not Facts

*How to share your experience without
forcing it on someone else*

I t's easy for people to disagree about today's hot issues, whether about politics, global warming, or social injustice. And then there are the smaller disagreements of everyday life, the little things, like setting the thermostat. Someone wants to turn it down. You want it up. Someone says "It's too hot in here." You say "It's not hot. It's cold!" Before you know it, you're in a silly argument. None of us need more aggravation, especially right now.

In order to express yourself respectfully and defuse arguments before they start, it's important to understand the difference between facts, opinions, and toxic opinions.

A *fact* is a thing that is known or proven to be true:

¤ The earth is round.

¤ Google is a search engine.

¤ Water is a simple molecule of positively charged hydrogen atoms and one large negatively charged oxygen atom.

An *opinion* is a view or judgment that depends on your assessment:

¤ I like pizza.

¤ I feel happy when I take a walk.

¤ I prefer to wear dark colors.

A *toxic opinion* is an opinion disguised as a fact:

¤ That project will never work.

¤   There's a worldwide shortage of jobs right now.

¤   There's no hope for a better life today.

Toxic opinions are problematic. When someone says, "It's too hot in here," it's easy to get defensive because the statement excludes any possibility that your experience might be different. The toxic opinion doesn't consider that you might be cold. "Too hot" is a relative term. It's not a universally accepted fact. It might be cute when a child says, "Brussels sprouts are gross." But it's not cute when adults confuse opinions with facts.

Opinions disguised as facts are toxic because they diminish the perspectives of others. Toxic opinions invite defensiveness and open the door for arguments; t is how many arguments start. One person imposes their opinion on someone else, and the other person aggressively pushes back, their opinion now turning toxic. "It's not hot in here. I'm freezing!"

When I teach this concept to my clients, I ask them to argue with me. "The room is hot!" I tell them. They say, "No, it's not. The room is fine. What's wrong with you, anyway?"

"Okay, good. Now, argue with this: 'I feel hot.'"

I get nothing but blank looks. No one can come up with an argument.

Someone can *disagree* by saying "I feel cold," but that's not *arguing*. They're just stating how they feel.

By saying "I feel hot," I'm merely describing how I feel and what I'm experiencing. I'm not suggesting everyone else should feel that way.

As I have mentioned earlier, "I" statements demonstrate personal ownership, accountability, and taking responsibility. By using an "I" statement, you can defuse an argument before it happens. Researchers from Australia have shown that "I" statements can reduce defensiveness and aggression.

Arrogance and believing one version of reality— yours—is the only possible view that underlies toxic opinions and could be the single largest creator of arguments.

Two types of toxic opinions

There are two types of toxic opinions: impersonal and personal. Impersonal would be something like:

- ¤ "Conservatives don't care about the poor."
- ¤ "Technology is ruining our lives."
- ¤ "Wealthy people are selfish."

On the other hand, personal toxic opinions include:

- ¤ "You're lazy and leave all the housework up to me."
- ¤ "You don't listen to me."
- ¤ "That's the stupidest idea I've ever heard."

You can rephrase a toxic opinion by saying "I think" followed by supporting facts or by stating what you experience and how you feel. Opinions and points of view—if grounded by the facts as you see them—are powerful, direct, and respectful ways to communicate.

It's empowering to say "Look, this is my opinion on the subject. You might disagree, but I want you to know what I think." For example, the statement "I feel hot. The thermostat says it's 75 degrees in here" expresses your experience and states a fact. So do these statements: "I think technology is ruining lives. I read a study from Harvard citing cellphone use by small children reduces cognitive brain function." "When we agree to sit down to watch TV together, and you get on your iPad, I feel disrespected and unappreciated."

Why opinions are necessary

The purpose of an opinion is not to prove someone wrong or convince them of your point of view. The goal is to speak truthfully and accurately about what you know or believe without discounting others' experiences. Without opinions, we would have no creative dialogue or problem-solving. We would be empty shells with little or nothing to say.

Instead of inciting defensiveness, an opinion should invite dialogue. You take responsibility for your point of view by saying, "I think," "I believe," "I propose," or "I suggest." When you use these words, you encourage others to do the same, although whether they follow your lead is up to them. You've done your part. Everyone is entitled to their opinion, and we all have the right to express our point of view. We might agree with each other, or we might not. But no one is entitled to impose their opinion on anyone else—whether about politics or the thermostat.

*   *   *

My wife, Mariclaire, and I have had numerous conversations about the thermostat in our house. She often feels hotter than I do, and we've had our moments. Now I wear an extra layer on cold days. She dresses more lightly. When she says "It's too hot in here," I smile and say "Oh, so you're feeling warm? Let's turn it down for a bit." She looks at me, laughs, and says, "Right, I am feeling warm." I smile because even though we both teach this stuff for a living, we don't always get it right. We're just human, after all. We are living, learning, and trying to be the best versions of ourselves that we can be.

We Behave Differently
Because We're Wired Differently

Here's why you might think someone
is impossible to deal with

A few years ago, when Mariclaire and I were dating, I was cooking dinner in her home and stopped to look for a knife so I could chop some vegetables. She told me to try the top drawer near the stove. When I opened it, I found a knife all right— along with a hammer, screwdrivers, a tape measure, a chunk of string, a small tube of glue, and lots of other stuff.

Her house was tidy; everything arranged just so—the plants, the artwork, all the little touches. Every day, she makes the bed, pillows arranged symmetrically. But when I opened the cabinets looking for a can of tomatoes—same thing. Everything was all over the place, as if she had just dumped the bag of groceries on the shelf.

Her outer environment was immaculate. Her inner environment was random and very different from mine. These fundamental differences between people can often create stupefying arguments about the most ridiculous things, leaving us scratching our heads, asking ourselves, "How is it possible they do that?"

But we're all wired differently, so we all behave differently. Yet we tend to think everyone else should think and act as we do. When they don't, we get annoyed and frustrated, and sometimes we argue, hoping we can change the behavior we find so perplexing and irritating.

How we see the world

According to Jungian personality theory, the way we show up in the world results from our three psychological preferences:

1. How we orient ourselves in the world and how we gain energy. Commonly known as introversion and extroversion.

2. How we make decisions. Do we make them more formally or more informally? Referred to as thinking and feeling.

3. How we take in and process information. Do we rely more on our five senses, known as sensation? Or do we rely more on our sixth sense, our intuition?

It's the last one that can explain Mariclaire's junk drawer: sensation and intuition.

When we take in and process information with a preference for sensation, we use our senses and focus on the here and now. When we process information using intuition, we take it in more imaginatively, focused on the future and what could be. Some people lean hard to the left, some to the right, and some find themselves more in the middle.

How we take in and process information

Sensation		Intuition
Specific	←———————+———————→	Global
Present-oriented	←———————+———————→	Future-oriented
Realistic	←———————+———————→	Imaginative
Consistent	←———————+———————→	Unpredictable
Down-to-earth	←———————+———————→	Blue-sky
Practical	←———————+———————→	Conceptual
Precise	←———————+———————→	General
Factual	←———————+———————→	Abstract
Step-by-step	←———————+———————→	Spontaneous

Source: Insights

Based on her attention to detail and practical approach to life, I thought Mariclaire preferred sensation when I first met her, but the more I got to know her, I learned she favored intuition even more. How stuff looks in drawers and cabinets is simply not of interest to her.

It's different for me. I'm very sensing. I organize my junk drawer with small boxes holding various bits and pieces. I'm damn proud of them, and if they get out of line, they get a tune-up.

I tried systemizing her cabinets when she was out one day. I bought some small baskets, cleaned everything out, arranged the new baskets—canned goods in one, flour in another—even labeled the shelves to provide further clarity. I stood back admiring my hand-iwork as if I'd figured out the cure for the common cold.

A week or two later, the cabinets were a mess. All my labeling tape fell off, too. I said, "Screw it," and gave up.

Sensation and intuition

People with a strong preference for sensation can easily pay attention to the details, especially if they are introverted. Their mind is like a photographic plate, picking up and retaining things like the expression on someone's face, the details of someone's clothes, the precise words they say.

When someone is more extroverted and sensing, they are likely to keep their environment neat and tidy (like me). They are rarely late for a meeting, they seek situations that stimulate their senses, and they have little patience for discussing abstract topics.

Sensing is the world of the here and now, the practical. Sensing wants to have a map, follow directions, understand the steps in a recipe, keep accurate notes, and have a tidy desk.

Intuition is the world of what could be. It's our sixth sense—the ability to pick up silent signals, see patterns, and make connections between seemingly disparate bits of information. Intuition is the ability to understand something instinctively without the need for conscious reasoning.

It's not uncommon for start-up founders to have a strong preference for intuition. They're looking for the next big thing, spotting the possibilities, and getting ideas started. Founders like that also need someone with a strong sensing preference around them to ground their vision in day-to-day operations.

People with lots of intuition can get lost in their daydreams, become forgetful, and can look lost to people with a preference for sensation. And they might get physically lost too, wandering about, exploring, adrift in thought, not interested in the practicalities of the world around them. Artists, musicians, and poets often have a great deal of intuition.

Intuition and sensation in everyday life

Intuition and sensation can show up in a lot of ways in our lives, such as:

Intuition	Sensation
• Doesn't care which way the toilet paper sits in the holder—new sheet from the bottom or top.	• Has a strong opinion about it
• Gets dressed to go out, not that concerned if things match	• Everything matches—belt, shoes, handbag, accessories. Hair coiffed immaculately.
• Figures out which way the bottom sheet fits the bed on the fly	• Puts a mark on one corner of the sheet to note which way the sheet goes. (When Mariclaire caught me doing this, she laughed in my face again.)
• Might follow a recipe once; after that, it's all improvisation.	• Follows the recipe and keeps following it precisely
• Prepares food in a free-flowing manner	• Chops vegetables precisely, placed in small staging bowls.
• To-do lists are kept mentally	• Has to-do lists, checks things off, and, if something gets done and is not on the list, will write it in and check it off

We behave differently because we're wired differently psychologically. Our preferences are like an invisible, silent guidance system continually operating below the surface and influencing what we think, say, and do.

*   *   *

The next time you're about to flip out or think someone is a jerk because they're doing something that makes no sense to you, remember that their preferences are probably quite different from yours. Take a deep breath and try to appreciate that what's inconceivable to you is normal for them.

Practical Tips for Type-A Personalities

Your strengths don't have to bite you in the butt

I f you're a type-A personality on a good day, you can be bold, determined, and achievement-oriented and get a lot of stuff done. On a bad day, you can be overbearing, critical, impatient, intolerant, and short-tempered. You can act like an ass, get in people's faces, and cause all sorts of trouble for yourself and others. I'm a Type A, so I know.

Trouble starts when:

- You are argumentative, stubborn, and hard to get along with.

- You interrupt people while they are speaking.

- You don't listen fully and jump to conclusions.

- You are too blunt, overly critical, or perfectionistic.

- You are excessively consumed with winning.

- You don't take criticism well.

- You present your opinions as facts.

- You raise your voice and get angry and aggressive.

If you aren't sure what personality type you are, imagine that each column of words below is a card. First, what card is most like you? Next, what card is least like you? Then, force-rank the remaining two columns.

If the fiery red card (type-A personality traits) sits on top, welcome to the Type A club. If it sits second, you're probably at least an affiliate member. To be your best, you, like me, have to keep the fire—

Cool Blue	Sunshine Yellow	Fiery Red	Earth Green
Cautious	Sociable	Competitive	Caring
Precise	Dynamic	Demanding	Encouraging
Deliberate	Demonstrative	Determined	Sharing
Questioning	Enthusiastic	Strong-willed	Patient
Formal	Persuasive	Purposeful	Relaxed

(Source: Insights Discovery Personal Profile)

what occasionally gets you in the doghouse but makes you great, too—under control.

What typically irritates Type-A personalities

Being told what to do. This is a big trigger for me because my basic personality resists authority. Fiery red energy wants to be in charge, not someone else.

Lack of focus. Because I'm task-focused with an eye on getting things done, if I'm interacting with someone who is all over the place, I can get irritated. Fiery red energy likes to be on point, on task, and focused.

Indecisiveness. I'm generally very decisive, so I'm not impressed if someone waffles, hesitates, or is unclear. If I'm not in a good place, I might get impatient. Fiery red energy likes precision, action, and moving things forward decisively.

Incompetence. Fiery red energy often views those who appear to be incompetent as getting in the way of completing a task. It likes being good at things. It appreciates being recognized for its ability to achieve and knows that it takes hard work to succeed. Incompetence can wind us up.

Being out of control. Because fiery red energy wants to control its external environment, if it finds itself in a situation with less influence or control than it would like, it can get uncomfortable and reactionary

(Source: Insights Learning & Development)

Tips to manage your fiery red Type-A energy

Slow down. We move quickly, think quickly, and want to get stuff done quickly. We write emails fast. How often have you written an email, and just before hitting Send, you go back to the beginning and insert, *Hello, I hope you are doing well.* We're goal-focused and want to crack on and climb the next mountain. Remember to breathe. Take some deep breaths every few minutes, and tell yourself, "You don't have to get everything done today."

Listen. Don't interrupt. When someone is speaking slowly or going in a direction already anticipated, you want to jump in, right? Your talkative mind is going nuts. You want them to shut up and finish. You want to tell them to hurry up. But don't say anything. Wait until they finish speaking. There's nothing more arrogant, irritating, or rude than somebody talking over someone else. Bite your tongue, breathe, chew on your fingernails, and do anything but interrupt.

Acknowledge, clarify, and confirm. Before making your point in a conversation, use active listening skills to acknowledge, clarify, and confirm.

¤ "So, let me see if I have this right. What's important to you is closing the deal before the deadline. Not waiting, correct?"

¤ "I'm not sure what you mean by 'intermittent failures.' Can you give me an example?"

¤ "Okay. Thanks for letting me know the draft proposal is on target. Now I have an additional question for you . . ."

Validate what you have heard. Be respectful of other people's opinions.

Stay present in conversations. You might get bored in meetings or conversations with your partner. Someone is droning on about something that you have little interest in. You decide to use the time to think about what's on your to-do list or what you're going to do after dinner. You drift off; you're half gone. Here's a suggestion: Find a way to stay present. Force yourself to look the other person in the eye. Be aware of your breath and bring all your attention to the conversation.

Use the check-in technique. A check-in is a great way for you to demonstrate your ability to connect on the human level before doing business. It will also help you and others get the most out of any meeting—whether it's with one person or in a group.

When people contribute and have a voice in a meeting, they feel more involved. More involvement means better outcomes. It also helps anyone running from one meeting to the next to get more focused. You can propose a few simple questions, such as,

¤ *How are you showing up today?*

¤ *What would you like to get from this meeting?*

¤ *What expectations do you have from our time together?*

Let each person briefly answer the questions while everyone else listens. No interrupting and no commenting. Set a time limit, if necessary. You might enjoy this free check-in generator, which provides dozens of check-in questions.

Practice verbal aikido. As mentioned in a previous essay, Aikido is a martial art that neutralizes an attack's energy without any offensive or defensive maneuvers. Instead of becoming reactive, verbal Aikido handles the attack by first standing your ground and using curiosity and inquiry before countering.

For example, if someone says "That's a dumb idea you have," rather than reacting defensively or aggressively, you might counter with "Oh, so you think it's dumb. I'd like to hear why you think so." This approach helps the attacker own and explain their opinion before you counter with an explanation of yours. It's disarming because they expect you to react negatively. When you don't, you've gained the higher ground.

Ditch arrogance for humility. Many people with Type-A personalities struggle with arrogance—believing that their ideas are foolproof, better, and more clever than anyone else's. They think that the way they do something is how everybody else ought to do it, but that's just arrogance disguised as trying to look smart.

When we're arrogant, we alienate people. Everybody thinks we're an ass—because we are.

Arrogance says "That project you're working on will never work."

Humility says "I have questions and concerns about the project you're working on. Can I share my thoughts with you?"

Arrogance presents its opinion as a fact.

Humility expresses its opinion as an opinion and is open and curious about alternative ways of thinking.

Let go of perfectionism and accept who you are—all of you. We're hard on ourselves. The inner critic can be brutal, and we expect to do everything right. When we screw up, we either deny it or replay it endlessly in our heads. We get angry at ourselves and get mad at the people around us—usually the ones we love the most. Then we wonder why we find ourselves alone, and we tell ourselves it's because we're the mad genius, and no one understands us. It's all bullshit.

We have to accept that we're not perfect. We're going to make mistakes, and others are going to make mistakes, too. Get used to it.

Learn to forgive yourself. Focus on learning, not doing everything right.

Practice mindfulness and/or meditation. As Viktor Frankl famously said, "Between stimulus and response, there is a space. In that space is our power to choose our response. In our response lies our growth and our freedom."

Being aware of our inner world is the key to managing our outer world. When we notice our thoughts and what is said or not said in a conversation, we can become more present. Instead of finding ourselves in a reactionary mode, we can find ourselves in an observing manner.

When we observe, we are less likely to get caught up in behaving badly. We have time to reflect—even if just for a second. That one second gives us time to decide what to say, what not to say, what to do, and what not to do. Mindfulness and meditation can help us stay more present.

Learn to sincerely apologize. If you have a lot of fiery red energy, you have a lot of personal power. You're likely a leader or someone who has achieved significant success in your life. Because you have a dynamic personality, you have considerable influence and impact on others. So, when you falter, one of the most powerful things you can do is apologize for your contribution to a breakdown you caused— even if the other person doesn't choose to apologize, too.

Take the lead. Don't pour more gas on the fire. It only takes one person to end an argument. Let that person be you. Own up. Do the right thing, always.

*　　*　　*

Having a Type-A personality and having a lot of fiery red energy is a gift, and it comes with the responsibility to use it wisely.

So, one more time, here are the tips to help make you more effective (and probably even more likable) while you continue to make the world go round and get shit done.

- ¤ Slow down.
- ¤ Listen. Don't interrupt.
- ¤ Acknowledge, clarify, and confirm.
- ¤ Stay present in conversations.
- ¤ Use the check-in technique.
- ¤ Practice verbal Aikido.
- ¤ Replace arrogance with humility.
- ¤ Let go of perfectionism and accept who you are—all of you.
- ¤ Practice mindfulness and/or meditation.
- ¤ Learn to apologize sincerely.

Forget About Trying to Change Someone's Mind

Instead, focus on what's in your control

I called my good friend William and left him a voicemail. "I'll be in Miami for five days," I told him. "Hope we can get together one evening." I never heard from him.

When I got back home, I called his mobile and work numbers. Nothing. I knew he was friendly with my ex-wife, so I asked her if he was okay. She said he was fine, but he was pissed off because I hadn't returned his call to me a month before my trip to Miami. I never got that call.

I reached out repeatedly for months to have a conversation. He wasn't having it. His mind was made up, and there was nothing I could do. I was stunned and disappointed.

Changing someone's mind in normal conditions is nearly impossible because of cognitive biases and heuristics, which are the brain's ability to invent quick mental shortcuts to solve problems and make decisions. It's even more pointless when we're emotional, under stress, or facing uncertainty.

Psychologically, we want stability, predictability, and normality—and when we experience something like the pandemic, the uncertainty of what might happen brings out our natural defense mechanisms. We're likely to hold on tight to what we believe will get us to safety. If we see a threat, we'll dig in even deeper. Beliefs get harder to change, especially when they are emotionally charged.

I felt the effects of raw uncertainty within me in 2020 and 2021. I was more easily agitated; bits of anger, anxiety, and frustration showed up more than usual. It made sense because the pandemic upended my lifestyle norms, and I had to readjust to a world of game-changing unknowns.

And it's not just trying to change someone's mind that's counter-productive. So is thinking about it obsessively, spending time devising clever ways to get through to them, and worrying about their decisions. For my own sanity, I've realized I have to rein in my ponies, call back the attack squads, and back off the accelerator.

It's not my job to change someone else's mind

I'm recommitting my energy and attention to activities that contribute to my overall well-being when it comes to things I can directly control, such as my thoughts, attitude, and behavior. Getting involved with anything I can't control, such as other people's behavior, the impact of the pandemic, or political decisions, is a waste of time and a big mood drain.

In *The 7 Habits of Highly Effective People,* Stephen Covey describes what we can and cannot control as "circles of concern and influence." We all have concerns—our finances, challenges at work, health, relationships with family and friends, the environment, and an unforeseen dangerous event. We care about all of them, but we have direct control over just some of them and not others.

When we focus on our circle of influence—that which is in our control—we become more positively energized and engaged. We step into our power, taking responsibility for our actions and choices. When we focus on issues outside of our circle of influence, such as someone else's political views, we can quickly get emotionally drained.

An exercise

A helpful exercise is to make a list of all the things you're concerned about. Then, replicate the diagram below on a piece of paper.

Place the items you can do something about in the smaller circle, namely, your Circle of Influence. Put the remaining items in the Circle of Concern.

Next, notice where you're spending your time and energy. If you're feeling agitated and down, you might be spending too much time in

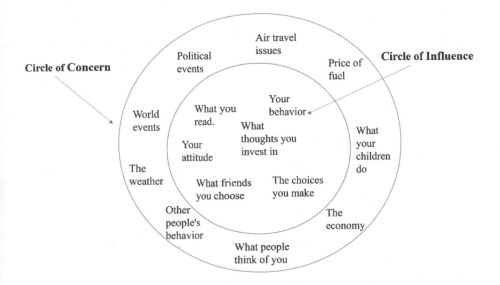

your circle of concern. The exercise might also help you realize your circle of influence is more significant than you think. There are many things over which you have control that make a significant, positive difference in your life.

Self-check

Eckhardt Tolle talks about catching yourself sooner when you get hooked, calling it one sign of spiritual growth. Given the current situation and challenges, it's a good time to ask yourself if you're staying poised and not getting hooked.

When I see myself getting reactive, I ask myself several questions:

¤ *What is the greater purpose of getting involved in this conversation? What is my intention?*

¤ *Is this within my circle of influence or not?* If not, I will do my best to let it go. Sometimes it's not easy. My ego wants to enlist my inner ninja and do battle. So, I take a deep breath and remind myself: It's not my job to change someone else's mind.

I'm trying hard to keep my attention on generative activities and choices that move me toward greater peace of mind, resolution, and acceptance of what I can and can't control. If I fail, I try to look at what happened and what I could have done differently. I might have to apologize or admit I was wrong. Sometimes it hurts because part of me likes to think I'm farther along the path than I am. But that's just the ego taking a good beating.

*   *   *

Uncertainty, as tough as it can be, reminds us that today's behavior creates the bed we sleep in tomorrow. Threats, guilt, and coercion don't win anyone's heart or mind. But behavior based on goodness will build a world that values kindness over vindictiveness, curiosity over arrogance, listening over judging, and respect over insults.

If people want to change their minds, they will. They just don't need us in their face.

How to Deal with Difficult People
Without Losing Your Mind

Don't wrestle with pigs, and don't die on every hill

When people are under stress, they are more likely to display a "bad day" version of themselves. Emotions close to the surface are easily triggered. When someone is stressed, angry, or irritated, they are less rational and empathetic, making the ability to resolve differences even more important.

What really matters in a difficult situation is how conscious and skilled you are. My former colleague Fred Kofman, author of the bestselling book *Conscious Business*, says: "There are no difficult conflicts. There are only conflicts we don't know how to resolve."

As an executive coach, I've helped leaders at major tech and financial companies learn conflict-resolution principles. Whether it's a conflict with family, friends, business colleagues, or the person who cuts in line at the grocery store, here is what I have found that works.

We all see the world differently

We each have a view of the world, and it's just that—our view. Others have their own views, which are likely different from ours. If I am self-absorbed, I believe my view of the world is correct, and everyone else is either wrong or badly misinformed. This is where many problems begin.

For example, if I'm a Democrat, I might believe I'm one of the good guys. Therefore, to me, Republicans are the bad guys, and I will likely discount anything a Republican says. I don't fully accept them or their point of view. Labeling someone as "bad" because I disagree with them is prejudice. This narrow-minded attitude has been the cause of wars, racial bias, political stalemates, religious persecution, and the destruction of entire cultures.

Resolving conflict begins with accepting that your point of view is just one version of the truth. There's always another story. Resolution is found through dialogue, not arguing about whose story is right, better, or more complete. Both stories are valid.

Accept duality: We're flawed and fabulous

Lisa Earle McLeod, in her superb book on conflict resolution, *The Triangle of Truth*, writes about seeing the world in binary terms. She calls it "either-or thinking." We categorize and judge people and things as "good" or "bad." When someone says or does something we disagree with, we often conclude they are wrong or manipulative. When we look through that filtered lens, it's all too easy to ignore, deny, or minimize their positive qualities.

While most of us are far less than perfect, we often find it difficult to accept the imperfections of others. If we want to be able to handle difficult situations, we have to accept that people can be both flawed and fabulous.

One of the most significant breakthroughs I've ever had was when I applied this principle to myself. Not only did I discover the healing power of full self-acceptance, I also found I was more accepting of others. If I am flawed and fabulous, can't others be this way, too? If I can be self-absorbed and loving, can't others be like this? If I am short-tempered and forgiving, can't others be like me?

Understanding the principle of duality allows us to be more open-minded when co-creating solutions to conflicts. We let go of harsh judgments, and we open our hearts and minds to improving the challenging situations we face.

Check your intent

No one wants to be steamrolled, beaten up, humiliated, or taken advantage of in an argument. And many of us don't want to do that to anyone else. While it might feel good at the moment to prove someone wrong, it doesn't improve the health of any relationship—business or personal. If you know you are heading into a potentially difficult situation or suddenly find yourself in one, ask yourself: What is my intention? Do I want to look good and be right, or do I want the best possible solution for everyone involved?

The root of many conflicts is the desire to be right and the need to defend one's position at all costs. But life is not about being right. It's about learning, growing, and making peace with ourselves and others.

If things heat up, get curious

When no one is listening during an argument, someone has to stop interrupting, tuning out, or discounting others. Let it be you. People think you gain control of a conversation by talking. You don't. You get control through inquiry and asking genuine questions because you are curious. To resolve a conflict, try to understand the other person's story and why they think the way they do. Here are a few things to say to help you do that:

- *"I'm struggling to understand what your real concern is."*
- *"Please tell me what makes you say that."*
- *"I must be missing something. Why don't you think the project will work?"*

According to research by psychology professor Albert Mehrabian, words only convey about 7% of the meaning in any conversation, while 38% comes from tone of voice and 55% from nonverbal communication. To help you hear somebody, listen for *how* something is being said in addition to *what* is being said. Notice body language and tone of voice. If you do that, you'll be able to pick up the story and emotions underneath the issue being argued.

When you recognize and acknowledge someone's emotional state, you're letting them know you're really paying attention. An operational or specific issue is more easily solved when someone's emotions are acknowledged first.

¤ *"I can see you are really, really frustrated and upset right now. You've got every right to feel that way, given the situation."*

¤ *"There's nothing more I want than for us to get through this peacefully. Help me understand what we can do to resolve this."*

Remember to breathe

If you can't listen to the person you're in conflict with, then the conflict will continue. Being aware of your breathing will help you get centered and increase your ability to listen. Breathe from your belly. Deep breathing from your belly will restore oxygen to your body and brain. Take as many deep breaths as you can. Slow the pace of the conversation. You've got to regain balance so that you can think clearly. It isn't easy to listen when you're flooded with emotion.

I did this recently, and it enabled me to stop arguing and become curious about what I heard instead of rejecting it. After doing that, the argument was soon resolved.

Learn to recognize the early warning signs that your emotions are taking over. If you feel your face getting red, your chest or throat tightening, or your body temperature rising, your reptilian "protect me from danger" brain has awoken. You've been triggered and are likely to go into a fight-flight-or-freeze response. The stress and survival hormone cortisol is in your bloodstream. Deep breathing will help you come back from the edge.

Speak honestly, respectfully, and accurately

Don't exaggerate or use grandiose statements such as "You always do that" or "You never do anything I ask." They are useless and inflammatory. Be specific and factual. Say what is true for you and state it that way. "I don't agree with that approach because . . ." Or "My concern about the project is . . ." Be accurate in your words.

Another part of speaking honestly is asking for what you want.

Many people struggle with making requests. Instead, they drop hints and expect others to magically figure out what they want. Or they make demands or ultimatums. None of those work well. If you want to improve your relationships, resolve conflicts, and stop blaming others, you have to learn to ask for what you want politely.

> "I suggest that before you decide to spend that kind of money, please speak to me first. Are you okay with that?"
>
> "I really need some quiet time now."
>
> "I propose that we split the cost on this one."

Be the first to apologize

If you screwed up, admit it—and do so with sincerity. There's nothing worse than a half-hearted, mock attempt at apologizing: "Yeah, sorry about that. I won't do it again." If you apologize from your heart, you're not only honest with yourself, but you are also letting the other person know you recognize your contribution to the situation. I have seen real apologies turn the tables entirely around in heated discussions.

Know when to disengage

If an argument is getting out of hand and emotions are running high on both sides, you have to make the call to continue or not. The reptilian brain is in charge, and it's all about survival—defend and attack. All head and no heart. What's the point? The only thing to do is to reduce the temperature. Someone must stop pouring fuel on the fire.

Call a timeout. Take a break. Reschedule when everyone is more clear-headed. Find a way to shift the energy; it can help. If you are sitting down, stand up. If you are standing, sit down. Avoid a situation where one person is sitting and the other is standing—be at the same physical level.

And remember, choose your battles carefully. Not every hill is worth dying on.

*   *   *

Life is a journey to be more conscious, loving, and compassionate. Along the way, we face challenges, and we grow as a result—learning to make wiser choices. When resolving a difficult situation, we can choose to do it thoughtfully with skill and kindness, or we can fight it out. The wiser choice is to use skill and kindness.

Eight Easy Things Extroverts Can Do That Introverts Love

*Being adaptable and flexible is essential
for better connections*

At every party, there are two kinds of people—
those who want to go home and those who don't.
The trouble is, they are usually married to each other.

—ANN LANDERS

As an executive coach, Jungian psychology practitioner, and extrovert married to an introvert, I can tell you that our differences don't just show up at the parties we attend. They show up in how we speak to each other, recover after a busy day, solve problems, and live day to day. Mariclaire often reminds me that—as an introvert—her world is quite different from mine. For that reason—and given that a third to a half of the world are introverts—extroverts can make a positive difference by connecting with our opposite type in the most considerate, inclusive, and respectful manner we can. I want to share what I've been learning. I hope it's helpful.

First, a few points to make sure we're all on the same page. There are many misconceptions about extroversion and introversion. "Introverts are shy, don't like to be in the spotlight, and have nothing to say." "Extroverts are loud, have nothing important to say, and are insensitive." None of these are universally true. Susan Cain, the author of *Quiet*, explains, "Extroverts really crave large amounts of stimulation, whereas introverts feel at their most alive and their most switched-on and their most capable when they're in quieter, more low-key environments."

The terms "extroversion" and "introversion" became more well known when Swiss psychologist Carl Jung researched and created a personality-type theory. Jung theorized that the primary distinction between our personalities is our orientation to the world, which will either be extroverted or introverted. They reflect our orientation to the world as well as how we gain and recharge our energy. Introversion and extroversion are preferences and can be thought of as being part of a continuum. No one is entirely an introvert or an extrovert; We all have characteristics of both. In other words, there are varying degrees of how much someone is introverted or extroverted. Jung also made it clear that we express both but prefer one over the other, if only slightly. That is our home base.

Differences between introverts and extroverts

In the magazine *Positive Psychology*, Elaine Houston writes, "Consider a busy social event. An extrovert will likely revel in the social interactions and be invigorated by it, while an introvert will likely find their energy depleted and need time alone to compensate." Extroverts speak to think. Introverts think to speak. Extroverts often use their speech to sort out their thoughts and ideas. Introverts go into their inner world to think and gain clarity. The thinking process is almost their version of speaking.

Introversion

Introverts are not all the same. There are two general types: thinking introverts and feeling introverts. Many thinking introverts work as engineers, scientists, and accountants, professions requiring thinking, analysis, and details. Feeling introverts often are attracted to roles involving people such as healthcare, customer support, human resources, or the nonprofit world. Thinking introverts are cautious, precise, deliberate, and formal, motivated by orderliness and correct processes. Feeling introverts are caring, encouraging, patient, and relaxed, motivated by harmony and a sense of fairness.

Introverts can be outspoken when discussing things that they're passionate about, but that usually only happens with close friends and family. They typically wait for others to initiate a conversation or to make friends with them. Privacy is crucial, and the sharing of personal information is limited. They will avoid conflict whenever possible and like being in others' company but not necessarily talking or socializing. Stressors include:

- ¤ Lack of information, structure, or logic
- ¤ Poor quality work
- ¤ Being rushed and pressured
- ¤ Unfair treatment or disregard for their values

Here's what extroverts can do when around introverts

1. Slow down

If you're extroverted, you likely walk, speak, think, and make decisions quickly. You are perhaps even mystified that everyone isn't like you. It feels so natural to be you, right? While others may think as fast as you do, they may not speak as quickly. If you want to connect more with an introvert, notice their speech pattern and adjust yours to be more similar.

Introverts may not do things as quickly as extroverts. An introvert might still be processing what just happened when an extrovert is off to the next task, agenda item, or new destination. You might have to slow down just a bit.

2. Be well prepared and thorough; put things in writing and provide details

Introverts like things to be organized and want to know what's coming their way so they can be well prepared. If you're meeting with an introvert, have your facts and details straight. Be specific and detailed, outlining outcomes and expectations. Don't be aggressive, short, or too direct—be friendly. If they write short, crisp emails, write the same way. Don't use emoticons unless they do.

3. Provide adequate time to answer questions

Introverts need time to process important decisions or difficult problems. They want to think, calculate, compare, and analyze. If you don't give them the time they need, you won't get their best. Putting an introvert on the spot for an immediate answer to an important question is equivalent to backing them into a corner. If you have something critical to discuss, give them advance notice, set a mutually agreeable time to speak, or send an agenda ahead of time and indicate what topics you want to discuss. Set them up for success.

4. Assume positive intent

I've sat in many meetings where people later complained that someone didn't say anything in the meeting. "Glenn never says anything. He waits for others to speak. Is he not on board with the strategy?" Glenn could be an introvert.

Destructive and false stories are often created when someone interprets another's behavior and compares it to group norms. So don't make the mistake of judging a quiet person as aloof or disinterested. Ask yourself, "What don't I know about this situation?" If you find yourself making up a story, develop the most respectful interpretation you can.

5. Invite them into conversations and listen

Introverts often wait for others to speak up first. They're listening, observing, and thinking. Invite them into conversations. Ask them, "Would you like to say anything?" Give them the option to speak up. Make room for them. It's almost unthinkable they would barge into a busy conversation.

When an introvert speaks, don't interrupt or finish their sentences. Extroverts, because of our bias for quickness, activity, and action, can become impatient and think we know where a conversation is going. A smarter approach would be to let your assumption go and be respectful. Besides, we don't get any smarter by speaking; we get smarter by listening.

6. Be patient and supportive

Extroverts tend to focus on getting things done, thinking about the impact on people later. How many times have you written an email, about to hit send, and then added, "Hi, how are you? I hope your day is going well." When we move so quickly, it's easy to forget others want to experience human touch. Taking the time to ask someone how they are doing before jumping into the business is respectful and sets a warm tone. Introverts want to know you care about them as a person. They want to be listened to and appreciated.

7. Respect personal boundaries and the need for privacy

When I was dating Mariclaire, I'd stay in her house for a week at a time, and I realized I wanted more space to hang my clothes. One morning, while she was at work, I found a wooden clothes stand at a local charity shop. It looked nice to me and was functional, too.

I brought it home and proudly set it up in the corner of the bedroom. I thought she'd be quite pleased. However, things didn't go so well when she came home that evening. I neglected to consider the bedroom was her personal space, her temple, and I had just planted a giant wooden phallus-like structure into it. I still can hear her, "Boundaries, Don! Personal boundaries!" The clothes stand went back to the shop by 9:00 a.m. the next morning.

Introverts are not interested in excessively sharing their personal details. Nor do they want you to fill their quiet world with your entire life story. Oversharing is exhausting for them.

It's generally not a good idea to get too close to an introvert you don't know. It's an invasion of their privacy. Hugging? Many introverts I know detest it unless it's from a close friend. An awkward A-frame hug from an introvert is all you need to know you hugged the wrong person. Give them space and respect their private nature.

8. Lower the volume when necessary

Introverts live in a much quieter world than extroverts. Loud voices and noise are disturbing. While we're thinking, "Why don't they say something," they're thinking, "When are they going to shut up."

I still get the occasional reminder from Mariclaire when watching TV for me to please turn down the volume. What a difference! While I'm having a great time, she's covering her ears. So, the volume goes down. No need to die on every hill. Happy wife—happy life.

The same goes for our voices. We may not realize how loud we sound to those who are quieter. If you have a loud voice, consider adjusting it down when necessary, whether you're at home, at the office, in a restaurant, or on an airplane. Introverts will appreciate it.

*   *   *

Life is all about connection—with ourselves and with others. When we pay attention to the unique style of introverts, we can better connect with them. Talking less, listening more, not interrupting, respecting boundaries, and not making assumptions is good common sense and will help. Doing the little things well makes a big difference between being tolerated and being likable.

Mariclaire just went for a walk, and it's time for me to take a break. I think I'll crank up some loud music.

Note: I have not included more information about introverts because there are plenty of books, like *Quiet* by Susan Cain, that are excellent resources for anyone with a preference for introversion. There is very little available for extroverts.

Turn an Argument with Your Partner into a Healing Conversation

Tips for recovering, healing, and resolution

My wife and I had a hot argument the other day. I got in her face about something she had agreed to do over the weekend. On Tuesday, it wasn't done yet. My irritation was building, and, in the middle of her busy workday, I brought up the subject. Bad idea.

Tip #1
The right conversation at the wrong time is the wrong conversation.

Mariclaire got quite angry at me and told me off, something she almost never does, so I knew the war drums were beating. I listened quietly and attempted a retort, but it wasn't well received. A better move would have been to zip my lips and say nothing. Not a good idea to continue the conversation when the fire is burning out of control. MC had to go back to work, and I had to leave the house for an appointment. It was just as well—we both needed to cool off. While it may be important to raise an issue, when you bring it up makes all the difference. ·

Tip #2
Don't pour more fuel on a burning fire. Deescalate it.

An hour later, we exchanged texts. She pointed out my tendency to overcontrol things, and I reaffirmed the importance of doing what we say we will do. We were still more interested in promoting our position than understanding each other's needs and concerns. I texted her: "Let's catch our breath and find our way to resolution and peace without blame. With love for you." "Yes, I agree," she said. "We can both do better! I love you too (mostly)!" Progress.

Tip #3
Someone needs to make a peace offering. Let that person be you, especially if you started the breakdown.

We reconvened at dinner. As we stared out the window and made small talk, tension filled the air. Finally, MC complained that I can over-egg the pudding and get too involved in things. She said it was chipping away at our relationship. I listened, as I tried hard to fully accept her point of view; I was struggling because I didn't see her making an effort to see *my* perspective. But that would come later. She first needed to download what she had been carrying.

Mariclaire and I had been married for almost three years by then. We both have fiery personalities and share deep spiritual beliefs, but we sometimes differ on some of the details of daily life—cooking, cleaning, how things look, what goes where, etc. For example, MC has high standards of household cleanliness; mine are not so high. She likes a quiet environment; I'm noisier. I like the contents of kitchen cabinets organized; she couldn't care less. For 30 minutes, we verbally danced back and forth, making some headway because we finally started to acknowledge each other's points of view. She needed to be heard, and so did I.

Tip #4
The more we feel heard, the softer our heart becomes. We become more receptive to different perspectives.

I realized I had disappointed MC in the past by not doing things she asked me to do—things I could have done, but I had been lazy. She reminded me how visual she is—that it's important to her that I wear something other than my same ratty blues jeans and shirt every day. We started to transition from arguing about and resolving operational issues to discussing our relationship and what was going on under the surface. It had been many months since we had discussed our relationship. As we talked, it became clear that both of us had been accumulating minor disappointments that were jamming up what would otherwise be a free flow of love, energy, and passion. This was resulting in irritation and resentment. Problems can only be solved when brought into the light. Left in the dark, they'll quietly become malignant.

I had wanted to have a conversation like that for a long time, and I silently hoped she would bring it up. If it's important to her, I thought, she would. But she didn't. But I didn't either. That was on me.

Tip #5
If you feel it, say it respectfully at the appropriate time and place. It's your truth. Better to speak it than bury it.

As we talked, we identified the parts of our relationship—the spiritual, physical, operational, values, interests, social, and emotional dimensions. We agreed that many are working well, and a few need more attention. It felt good to break down our relationship into its unique parts. It's easy in moments of frustration to lump everything together and claim the entire relationship sucks. But that's just a cop-out. Being specific about what is or isn't working clarifies what to keep doing, start doing, or stop doing.

As we closed the conversation, this is what we landed on: I need to make more effort to step up my everyday appearance around the house. I do a great job when we go out—hair washed, face shaved, clean, hip clothes. But, around the house? Not so much. She's visual and wants to be sexually attracted to me, so if I look unkempt, it's a turn-off. Through the conversation, I realized how important this is to her—and I told her I would step it up.

Me? I apologized for my bad timing and requested we keep our commitments to each other, big or small. She accepted the apology and agreed to my request. We talked about the value of time apart, something we haven't had much of since Covid. So, my two-week trip out of the country would be an excellent opportunity for us to have some space and reflect on what we could do differently.

We also took a free love language assessment at www.5lovelan-guage.com and discussed our results. It's another excellent way to talk about your relationship safely and positively.

Tip #6
Have a relationship health check conversation with your partner. Do a balanced assessment. Discuss what parts of the relationship are working or not.

We finished the conversation, cleaned up the kitchen, and a few hours later, went to bed, slipped beneath the covers, and rediscovered the magic. Loving, intoxicating, sublime.

*   *   *

Disagreements and breakdowns with your partner can happen. I love what Paulo Coelho said: "Not all storms come to disrupt your life; some come to clear your path."

PART 4

Living a More
Fulfilling Life

Five Signs You Are Making
the Most of Your Life

What I learned from 100 people over 50

"Wisdom comes with age" is not just an aphorism. Life experience is one of our greatest teachers. As we move through our lives, we accumulate wisdom about who we are, what's really important, and how we can live productively and happily. With this in mind, I recently polled about 100 people over the age of 50 for advice about making the most of life. I studied their comments, looking for the particular mental attitude or belief underlying each one. I found common patterns, used some reverse engineering, and distilled my findings into five signs that someone is making the most of their life.

Sign 1: You know you are a work in progress.

As a business coach, I've had the privilege of working with some brilliant clients. In 2008, I met Larry Tesler, an iconic figure in computer science. Larry attended Stanford University at the age of 16, joined Steve Jobs at Apple in 1980, and eventually worked with Amazon and Yahoo. He contributed significantly to early programming languages. When I met Larry, he was 62, and I was teaching a leadership development course at Yahoo. He was as curious and hungry to learn as the rest of the (much younger) people in the course. Even in his 60s, Larry knew he wasn't done growing. He was open, curious, and humble, and his enthusiasm was touching.

> *The secret of genius is to carry the spirit of the child into old age,*
> *which means never losing your enthusiasm.*
>
> —ALDOUS HUXLEY,
> English writer and philosopher

Believing you are a work in progress means you don't give up on yourself, thinking you can't change. You don't say, "That's just the way I am, and there's nothing I can do about it." Anyone can change and grow as long as they are intentional about it. When you believe you are a work in progress, you seek out ways to grow and improve. And, if you want to grow, you must work to understand any blockages or wounds in your past. Healing them is an essential step toward change and transformation.

I began diligently working on myself when I was 40. I read Debbie Ford's book, *The Dark Side of the Light Chasers,* and Robert Johnson's *Owning Your Own Shadow.* I joined men's groups, went to therapy, studied, journaled, meditated, did Holotropic Breathwork®, and went on sacred medicine journeys.

I dealt with perfectionism, insecurity, guilt, shame, spiritual ego, and childhood wounds that were all playing out in some way in my life, hindering my ability to be at my best. I made progress, but even to this day, there's still work to do. The more I realize I'm a work in progress, the more I realize everyone else is, too. I judge less and accept more. Life is more enjoyable when it's opened up by this perspective.

What work you do is up to you. The important thing is to do it and keep doing it. As one survey respondent said: "See reality as it is, not as you want it to be."

Sign 2: You pay attention to your inner world.

Paying attention to your inner world—your thoughts and feelings—frees you from being bound by them. The more you notice your thoughts, the more you realize you aren't your thoughts. When you don't pay attention to them, you go on autopilot and sleepwalk, and you can't notice the messages coming from your body, mind, and spirit because you're too distracted by everything around you. It's too easy to be preoccupied with the past and future, worrying about both.

When you pay attention and manage your inner world, you can make better choices. You're more resilient and can recover from difficulties more quickly. You can better manage your outside world. You make smarter life and business decisions. You respect differences, honor dissenting points of view, listen with empathy, and seek to be of service. When you pay attention to your inner world, you "learn to be in the moment," as one person I polled noted.

Sign 3: You live "above the line."

Think of the "line" as a division between being powerful and being powerless. Living above the line means accepting your power. When you live above the line, you know you have the ability to make choices, to choose your attitude and your behavior. You don't blame others or seek out scapegoats. You're forthright, honest, and direct, yet you avoid being rude or arrogant. You "learn to say no and have boundaries," a respondent added.

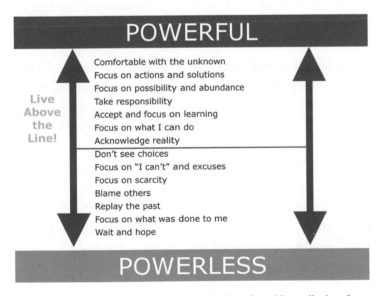

Image by the author with contributions from
Insights L&D and the Conscious Leadership Group

When you live "below the line," you complain, blame others, make excuses—and become powerless. You open the door to bitterness and regret. When our power isn't our own, we do things to please others, to fit in and be liked. We wind up marginalizing ourselves and losing our sense of self. People who carry that over a lifetime wind up insecure, unhappy, and resentful.

Living above the line puts you in the driver's seat of your life. It opens you up to a learner's mindset. You're curious and thoughtful, and you want to learn from your successes and mistakes. You take calculated risks. As one person put it, you "don't settle for mediocrity." You're not afraid to fail. You live with your arms open, pursuing everything you are capable of.

Sign 4: You do the right thing—even when it's hard.

Doing the right thing is not always easy. Sometimes it's painful. You might need to have a difficult conversation, fire someone, say No to a valued client, or walk away from a lucrative business deal because it compromises your values. I've had to do all these things, and after I did them, I knew I did the right thing.

When you're clear on what your highest values are, it's easier to make the right choices. Your highest values are defined by what you really care about. Ask yourself, "What's really important to me?" For some people, it's family or their faith in God. For others, it's being kind to others, honoring their word, or being honest.

For me, when I honor my highest values, I feel proud of my behavior. I'm at peace with myself because my behavior is in sync with what I believe. Therefore, our personal values are an internal safety net, supporting us when we are under pressure and flooded with stress hormones, unable to reason. There is no second-guessing, no little voice in our heads nagging us to do the right thing.

Telling the truth, honoring your word, standing up for yourself, or voicing your opinion even when you know it might be unpopular sets you free. As one respondent said, "You listen to the whispers of your soul."

Sign 5: You put your heart into what you do.

Bringing your heart with you means putting your full self into everything you do. You strive to be your best, no matter what the task is or who may or may not be watching. You care about yourself, your health, and your body, and you care about those around you. You seek to be proud of how you behave more than worrying about how you are perceived. People will remember when you live from your heart.

Your heart is curious. It wants to know how others think and feel. Your heart yearns for you to be gentler and more forgiving to yourself and others. It wants you to take care of your body and health. Your heart says "Thank you for another day of life" when you close your eyes at night. In the words of some of the people I polled, you "enjoy the journey," "find your passion," "follow your arrow," and "seize the day." Your heart is the best friend you'll ever have.

* * *

Life is not always easy; hard times are inevitable. But when you live life from the inside out, you're able to make better choices and live with your arms wide open, fully accepting what comes in return. Eckhart Tolle said it well: "If you get the inside right, the outside will fall into place."

Seven Habits to Keep You Vibrant

The time to build them is when you're
a young whippersnapper

I'm 70 now, and life isn't what I thought it would be—it's way *better*. In my 50s and 60s, I had my share of personal and professional challenges, but now I'm more peaceful, vibrant, productive, and committed to doing my part to help the world be a better place. That's what this article is about—seven habits that have contributed mightily to my well-being. Of course, you can get on board with these at any age, but if you're young and they become part of your daily routine, they'll likely serve you well as you get older.

1. Develop a mindset of abundance.

Worrying about money at any age is a drag, but you sure don't want to be worrying about it as you get older. When you're younger, the smart things to do are to invest wisely, live within your means, and stay as debt-free as possible. But you can do all that and still be a mental wreck.

The real game-changer consists of having an abundant mindset on financial, spiritual, mental, emotional, relationship, and work dimensions. With an abundant mindset, you know deep inside that your needs are being satisfied and will continue to be fulfilled. So, there's no need to struggle; you simply need to make an effort toward your goals and have unwavering trust and faith that your needs will be satisfied.

I didn't understand the mechanics of abundance until a few years ago, and I wish I'd paid more attention to it when I was younger. It would have eliminated a lot of unnecessary worrying and stress. Two things that helped me develop my mindset were doing inner transformation through holotropic breathwork and rewiring my brain through repeated listening to Deepak Chopra's 21-Day Meditation Experience. These experiences removed negative thought patterns and replaced them with an understanding that I don't just have enough; in fact, I don't have to struggle anymore. It was profoundly liberating, and it freed up stuck psychic energy that I now use for creative purposes.

Key point: A life of abundance begins with how you think. The sooner you can embrace abundance, the better.

2. Take good care of your spirit.

Someone recently told me they're never fully present—their mind is always racing all over the place, all the time. When I heard this, I recalled that my mind had also been running rampant before I began my meditation practice 50 years ago. I've now built a consistent, effective practice that tames the wild horses in my head, allowing me to tap into a beautiful experience of stillness and peace within.

Building a mindfulness or meditation practice is no different from exercising regularly—you build strength and develop a habit that will serve you throughout your life. If you commit to staying in shape when you're younger, for example, it's no big deal to keep it going when you're 70. The same applies to taking care of your spirit. Mindfulness or meditation might not be for you; perhaps you do something else that nurtures your spirit. But if you don't do anything, now is the time to start.

Key point: A consistent inner practice nurtures your spirit, bringing peace and joy through good times and bad. The older you get, the more you'll appreciate it.

3. Have goals.

I've always had goals in my life—I wanted to learn to play guitar, win a tennis championship, find the love of my life, and get promoted. Goals create a sense of purpose, a focus, and a feeling of pride and accomplishment when achieved. Now, I'm finding goals are as important as ever because I'm thinking more about what kind of mark I want to leave in the world, my legacy.

When I was younger, my goals reflected what I wanted to accomplish, minus the legacy part. Thinking about your legacy can take your goals to a whole new level and bring out your deeper and perhaps unconscious aspirations to make a significant difference. So why not think about your legacy when you're young?

Key point: No matter what age you are, goals help keep you focused, engaged, and motivated. Thinking about your legacy can take your goals to another level.

4. Take care of your body.

If you don't have good health, it's difficult to have an active life. We take a lot for granted when we're younger, as if we'll never wear out. I sure did. As an athlete, I pushed my body hard but took care of it as best I could. Over the past 10 years, I've upped my game and feel better than ever. I'm still six feet tall, 165 pounds, and can slip into the patched-up jeans I wore in college. And, for what's it worth, I haven't been sick in over 15 years—not a cold, not the flu, nothing. Knock on wood. What works for me might not work for you, but here's how I take care of my body.

No dairy and virtually no processed foods or refined sugar

Organic fruit and vegetables as much as possible

Practice Yoga regularly to maintain flexibility. Lift weights twice a week to maintain strength

Limited alcohol intake. Plenty of filtered water and herbal tea.

More skincare, especially the face

Walk, play tennis, or golf regularly

Daily doses of vitamins with an emphasis on vitamins D and C

Get plenty of sleep. Regular 16 to 18-hour fasts.

Key point: Treat your body with care and love. You'll want as much health as you can as you age.

5. Do work that is enjoyable, meaningful, and of service.

Enjoying what you do creates positive energy that nourishes the body, mind, and soul and brings creativity, joy, and optimism to your life. Sure, there are times in life when we need to take a job just for a paycheck. But if you're on stable ground and in a situation you don't enjoy, don't settle. Listen to your self-talk. Is your inner dialogue helping you move ahead or hindering you? What beliefs are you holding? Knowing what you want and shedding any limiting thought patterns are critical to finding work you enjoy.

Long-term health and happiness are functions of a healthy, satisfied mind, and enjoyable work contributes significantly to inner peace. At 70, I'm not interested in "retiring." I'm clear on what work I choose to do. If it doesn't fit the criteria of being enjoyable, meaningful to me, and of service to others, I don't do it. If it does, I'm all in.

Key point: Define what's important to you. Don't settle for good enough. Draw boundaries and say no to what doesn't energize you.

6. Choose your company wisely. Emotions are contagious.

Whether at work, with friends, family, or your lover, relationships either light you up or drag you down. The emotions of others are contagious, so knowing your boundaries is essential if you don't want relationship drama. My mental, emotional, and spiritual health is, in large part, directly related to the relationship I have with my wife. We love each other, share the same values, and are committed to doing ongoing inner work. Of course, there are times we trigger each other, too, and we have to work through what comes up. But that's all part of continuous growth and learning.

I try my best to approach all my personal and business relationships with the same attitude I have with my wife: I'm willing to listen to different points of view, committed to reducing tensions if they arise, and quick to forgive my failings as those of others.

My policy on people is simple: I only invest in relationships with pleasant people.

Key point: If you want peaceful, loving relationships in your life, commit to doing your inner work and bring humility, love, and compassion to all your relationships.

7. Be friendly, kind, and grateful.

The older I get, the more I realize that the way I treat myself impacts how I treat others. I've been tough on myself over the years, but now I'm much more forgiving of myself when I make a mistake or drift temporarily off track. That translates into being more compassionate and tolerant of people with whom I have an issue. Less drama and aggravation means more positive, vibrant energy flowing. When you're happy and at peace with yourself, it's easy to be with others. They feel your energy and want to hang out with you. It's not that complicated. It's the little things that count—being friendly to people in the shops you frequent, taking an interest in their world, listening more than you talk—this stuff matters.

And here's what I have to say about gratitude. It's not a buzzword or some trendy "New Age" thing. When we're grateful, we're in touch with our heart—our Higher Self. We tap into our chi, our life force. When we do this, we heal ourselves. It's like drinking from the fountain of youth.

I practice gratitude as much as I can, from the moment I open my eyes in the morning until I close them in the evening. It's energizing and keeps me humble and in awe of being alive—the ultimate gift, regardless of my circumstances.

Key point: Being friendly, big-hearted, and grateful allows you to express your humanity. The more you express it, the more alive you feel.

* * *

I don't know what life has in store for me, but I want to make the most out of it while I'm here. These seven principles help keep me full of life and love.

What is the Best Way
to Slowly Ruin Your Life?

*The value of a healthy mindset, self-awareness,
and taking care of your health*

No one wants to ruin their life, but some people manage to do it anyway. The definition of "ruin" is to "damage irreparably," and I've seen doctors, attorneys, and promising young writers self-destruct as a result of unmanaged bad habits, drug and alcohol abuse, and illegal behavior. When we see it happen, whether it's a celebrity or someone we know, we're often surprised, but when we look closer, it's usually been a slow burn all the way down.

A question began to intrigue me: "What is the best way for someone to slowly ruin their life?"

The word "slowly" adds a provocative nature to the question—if something takes place over time, there is a chance to catch it, reverse it, or stop it before it's too late. Imagine a pencil rolling slowly across a table toward the edge. You can see it; you know it's going to fall. You can grab it and save yourself the trouble of bending over to pick it up once it lands on the floor, or you can just let it continue rolling until it's gone over the edge. In Hemingway's *The Sun Also Rises*, a character is asked, "How did you go bankrupt?" The character answers, "Two ways. Gradually, then suddenly."

So I asked my friends on Facebook and my contacts on LinkedIn, "What is the best way for someone to slowly ruin their life?" Within minutes of posing the question, I received over 100 replies. The responses seemed to fall into three categories: having a negative mindset, lacking self-awareness, and ignoring mental, physical, or spiritual health. Here are several representative entries:

A negative mindset

- ¤ Be cynical.
- ¤ Blame others for one's behavior.
- ¤ Look at everything you don't have.
- ¤ Have a harsh inner critic.
- ¤ Worry about the past or future.
- ¤ Let fear run your life.

Lacking self-awareness

- ¤ Have no interest in your inner world.
- ¤ Be unable to slow down.
- ¤ Lie to yourself.
- ¤ Ignore your intuition.
- ¤ Allow others to define who you are.
- ¤ Constantly focus on gratification from your outside world, which you think you can control.
- ¤ Link your happiness to others' perceptions and expectations of you.

Ignoring mental, spiritual, and physical health

- ¤ Eat "unhealthy" foods.
- ¤ Ignore your body's natural cues.
- ¤ Try to escape into addictive behaviors.
- ¤ Get into toxic relationships.
- ¤ Put yourself in compromising situations.

Obviously, if you don't want to ruin your life, then do the opposite of everything listed above. But I wanted to get below the surface and uncover the mindset, attitudes, and beliefs that underlie destructive behavior patterns. Here are a few strategies that can help make sure you don't ruin your life. Or, if you do get off course, they can help you get back on track.

Face the brutal truth

Denial is dangerous. When we're hiding from something we don't like—whether it's some part of ourselves or the situation we're in— we invent distractions. We escape confronting the issue by anesthetizing ourselves with activities that initially appear harmless but take on a destructive life of their own.

For example, we can deny our toxic relationships or convince ourselves our compulsive behavior or addiction is just temporary—even if we know these are unfulfilling forms of escape. Left unchecked, excuses become ingrained habits that are detrimental to our well-being.

When I've found myself on the wrong path, the turnaround began by facing the brutal truth. Without that, nothing would have changed. Accepting our circumstances as they are, looking in the mirror, and admitting what is happening are the first steps to breaking the cycle of denial.

Putting things off, minimizing the impact of unhealthy habits, and convincing ourselves there is some redeeming benefit to what we are doing, while you know full well it's not good for us, is flat-out denial—"lying to yourself," as one person described it. You might want to ask yourself, "What am I allowing in my life that is no longer good for me?"

Summon courage

Facing what you don't want to deal with is not easy at first. There is courage within us; we have to find and make friends with it. I found courage through prayer, asking for help, and looking deep within my heart to find my courage. The heart knows what is right and can be our inner guidance system. The heart doesn't care about the future or the past. It only cares about what is best for you and doing the right thing.

When we face challenging situations, it's often necessary to make hard choices. To get what we want, sometimes we have to let go of something significant. For example, if you choose to leave a marriage with children, you're aware that the change in the structure of the family unit will be difficult, but the reasons to do so are more critical than keeping it intact. That is not an easy decision to make. You must summon your courage to do the right thing.

Enter your cave

The "cave" is our inner world. It's the part of us that contains our fears, false beliefs, lies, guilt, and shame. When we first enter the cave, we're usually afraid of what we will find in the shadows and darkness. Courage lights the way and steadies us as we go deeper into ourselves. It's not unusual to find a guide, a friend, or a mentor to offer assistance on the journey.

When you pay more attention to your inner world, it's not uncommon to become more observant of your outer world. You might notice things you've previously missed that now have significant meaning. I found myself discarding the concept of "coincidence" when explaining a random meeting with someone who offered me invaluable help. I replaced it with the understanding that the Universe is looking out for me. Once you start doing more inner work, entering your cave, help often appears in new and seemingly unusual ways. The more present and self-aware you are, the more you can recognize the gifts being given to you.

Sometimes we think we don't have the power to be the person we want to be—but we do. That person exists within us, hidden in the shadows, waiting to come out. The darker our cave gets, the brighter the light will be on the other side.

Know what you want

Knowing what you want in life incites movement toward the vision. Without knowing what you want, how can you move toward it?

Create a vision for yourself. It might be as simple as, "I want a loving relationship," or "I want to have a life of abundance." Don't under-estimate the power of intention. The details are not necessary at this point. What is essential is freeing yourself from being held captive by false stories and limiting beliefs.

*   *   *

The stories you tell yourself make or break you. Tell yourself you are amazing, you're good, you deserve everything possible, you want the best that life has to offer, and there is nothing—nothing at all—that can stop you.

Top Secret:
Guides for a More Meaningful Life

If it feels like the world is crumbling,
it's time to look inward

Now, more than ever, we need to find our strength, courage, and fulfillment from within. Real contentment is not—and never has been—a result of other people, places, and things. It's within us, and there are practical ways to experience it. Here are principles that can help achieve it:

Have a regular inner practice

There might be nothing more important than having a practice that connects us to our Higher Self. Meditation allows us to experience our essence, the universal life energy within us. When we do this, we understand we aren't our thoughts, ideas, or beliefs: We are consciousness. We become the observer of our thoughts and the questioner of our beliefs. We don't grow when we're not paying attention. Meditation is practical. If you learn correctly and stick with it, the results can be life-changing.

Strive for balance

I was born with a fiery temperament, which has been a blessing and a curse. It's been instrumental in my business career, driving me to achieve and perform. But I've gotten into many jams by reacting too quickly, judging, criticizing, and arguing, especially when I'm under stress.

I've learned I can "dial up" the part of me that's more sensitive, caring, considerate, and people-focused—opposite yet complementary qualities to the task-driven, fiery energy I was born with. When we integrate opposites, we can be both powerful and compassionate, bold and kind, purposeful and caring, strong-willed and patient, demanding and collaborative.

This principle of balance is well expressed in the Chinese philosophy of Taoism. Yin and yang represent two halves of our being that form wholeness. Yin and yang are interdependent and flow into each other. Imbalance exists when there is an excess or lack of either one. Being in balance enables us to access our full power; we are naturally more self-aware and can flex and adapt situationally.

Use and trust your intuition

Our analytic and methodical traits are mostly sourced in our left brain, whereas our artistic and creative traits belong to the right brain. Thinking and planning are more "left-brain" qualities, and intuition and spontaneity are more "right-brain" qualities. According to Jungian psychology, our brains also have two fundamental decision-making functions: thinking and feeling. When we make decisions, we tend to use one function first and back it up with the other.

One way to be more conscious is to lean into your intuition if you don't use it enough. Highly developed intuition is a "secret weapon," says Judith Orloff, author of *Guide to Intuitive Healing* and professor of psychiatry at UCLA. "It gives you all kinds of information you wouldn't normally have. This isn't the brain analyzing; this is nonlinear knowledge. It's a second kind of intelligence. You want to use both."

Here's how you can tap into your innate intuition:

¤ *Trust your gut.* We've all heard it—and it's true: We need to pay attention to our gut. The gut houses neurotransmitters, and when we pay attention to our gut, we notice if we feel at rest or uneasy. Stress often manifests as tightness in the chest, stomach, or throat, so if you don't feel at ease when you're making a decision, heed the message.

¤ *Pay attention to moments of inspiration.* Intuition often appears in flashes. You might get a jolt, a thought, an idea—almost like a download. "Oh! I just realized that I know someone who can help with . . ." Notice those. If you can't act on them right away, write them down.

¤ *Make time for reflection.* Build time into your day for a few minutes of silence. Disengage from all your electronic devices. One way to reflect is to close your eyes and notice any sensations in your body. Then continue with 10 deep breaths, followed by gentle slow breathing. Pay attention to your breath, relax, and observe any thoughts or feelings. Another way to reflect is to write down what you are most aware of: thoughts, feelings, emotions.

¤ *Observe your feelings.* Pay attention to the levels of energy you have. Notice how you react when you think of someone you have to call. Do you feel excited and energetic about the call? If not, your intuition is telling you something. Find out what that is all about. Chances are, there is something unresolved.

Be Curious

When we are more curious, we become more conscious. We realize we don't know everything. We're willing to suspend the belief that the way we see the world is the only truth. We're intrigued and appreciate the mysteries of life. Before you judge someone or something, ask yourself, "What don't I know about this?" A closed mind can't be fully conscious. An open mind can be more conscious.

Being conscious means to be awake—to be aware of one's inner and outer worlds. When we aren't paying attention to our inner world, we miss what we need. We won't grow, and a richer, fulfilled life will slip through our fingers.

Face and speak the truth

We have to clean what needs cleaning. To be more conscious, we can't live a double life or a life full of half-lies. We can't have a relationship with one foot out the door or be partially committed to our work. We can't have unresolved issues with people because we are afraid to speak the truth. When we face our shadow, we are on the way to being more conscious. Once we identify the ways we're not in harmony, the real work begins; and most of the time, it involves telling the truth. When we do that, we set ourselves free. Our consciousness will rise, and we will feel whole and more at peace.

Some years ago, I was in a relationship that had become fractured. I maintained it, rationalizing that it was "good enough." I avoided facing the truth that I wanted it to end, and I suffered quietly. Eventually, I found the courage to speak up, and the weight of silence disappeared. A new, more harmonious life began, and the doors of being conscious opened wider.

Choose your company wisely

Spending time with people who are unconscious and generate negativity will gradually infect you. I've had to walk away from people and environments that no longer served me, learning it was okay to disappoint someone else in service of taking care of myself. Be discriminating about who you associate with because their energy and belief systems will influence you. We absorb messages from everything around us. Surround yourself with more conscious people, and the impact will be empowering.

Listen to and take care of your body

The more I've practiced being more conscious, the more I pay attention to taking care of my health and my body. For example, for many years, I had to clear my throat. I had plenty of colds and nasal congestion and believed it was normal. Then I decided to stop eating dairy foods, and within weeks, the congestion disappeared. I had been ignoring my body, not realizing it was telling me something was out of balance. It turned out that I had an undiagnosed dairy allergy.

Our bodies hold valuable information, and when we pay attention, we can pick up the messages. Being in balance emotionally, mentally, and spiritually promotes a healthy body. Disease comes from not being in balance. In *You Can Heal Your Life*, Louise Hay writes about the mind-body illness connection and how we can heal ourselves through releasing negative emotions like resentment, criticism, and guilt. If you know someone filled with negative emotions, notice if they appear healthy, happy, and balanced. It's likely they do not.

Question your own beliefs

Our lives are the result of our behavior, our choices, our natural hard wiring, and the actions we take. Our belief systems and what we think underpin and drive what we do. If you change your thoughts and change your beliefs, you change your life. The ability to question your beliefs takes self-awareness, willingness, and courage. When you are observing your beliefs, you can reduce the habit of identifying with them. When you stand outside of something, you can change it. We can change our thoughts from "I'll never be able to do this" to "I haven't been able to do this—yet."

Practice gratitude

When we are grateful, we tap into the part of our brain most responsible for happiness. It's the same part of the brain that is activated when we meditate. No matter what challenges you face, reminding yourself of what you are thankful for is a powerful way to disengage from negative thinking and connect to the greater good. Before you go to sleep and when you wake up are two ideal times to do this.

Be courageous

It takes courage to try to be more conscious and walk what Zen Buddhism calls the "middle path." We might be alone in this pursuit and criticized by others who don't understand or disagree with what we are doing. The messages we get from the world don't encourage us to be more conscious. Whether watching a sports event on TV or looking at magazines in a shop, we are encouraged to drink more beer, eat more burgers, and climb the corporate ladder. We have to be willing to go against popular opinion and be ready to be misunderstood. The path you are on is invisible to anyone else—*it's your path for a reason.*

*   *   *

As I've continued to use these principles, my life has gradually blossomed, and I've grown in ways I never imagined. I'm more creative, empathetic, fulfilled, and happier in my relationships. I worry less, laugh more, sleep better, and rarely get agitated. When I find myself going off the rails, I catch myself sooner, and I recover faster.

The learning continues. I am still peeling away new layers of psychic debris, making mistakes, and wandering off track. I still smile at my moments of unconsciousness, which happen regularly. They remind me that I'm still curious and still learning. Living life with arms wide open and going for what I know to be true for me has been worth every single effort.

I hope your arms are wide open, too, and you find real happiness and meaning within.

The Importance of Feminine Energy
in a Male-Dominated World

When we become more whole, we usually bring more goodness

We are born into a world of opposites. Dark, light. Hot, cold. Summer, winter. Right brain, left brain. Yin, yang. Masculine, feminine.

All people have masculine and feminine energy, which has nothing to do with biology, sexuality, or gender. There are positive, bright, or mature expressions of both masculine and feminine energies, as well as immature, dark, or toxic expressions of them.

For example, women can be purposeful, strong, and driven. While our culture defaults to associating these qualities with men, that's a superficial interpretation of what's happening. These traits are actually just the healthy expression of masculine energy; it doesn't matter who's doing the expressing. On the flip side, traits that are often associated with femininity—such as being sensitive or kind—are not exclusive to women. Men can be kind; men can also be tough—as can any person of any gender. What's most powerful—and most attractive—is when someone can be both.

We each have our part to play if we want a better world. As a man, I'll speak to what I see as our potential to contribute to a brighter future.

Men hold most of the power and wealth in the world. Because of this, we can make a unique contribution by understanding and realizing our full potential. Full potential means accessing all parts of ourselves—those familiar, like our masculine side, and those perhaps less familiar, like our feminine.

When we overdo the most familiar parts of our psyche and neglect those parts of ourselves that create balance, we create problems for ourselves and others. Being out of balance opens the door to our psyche's darker elements, leaving us stressed out, angry, bitter, resentful, or vindictive.

The alternative is integration and wholeness. The joining of opposites creates wholeness. This occurs when we integrate and manifest our positive masculine and feminine energy. When we become more complete as human beings, we're apt to bring more goodness into the world.

While we all benefit from the many significant contributions made by men and women throughout history, men are, sadly, responsible for most of the evil. Wars, genocide, mass shootings, rape, and abuse primarily result from men—unconscious men, men consumed with toxic masculinity. Every day, this twisted masculinity shows up as hostility, aggression, arrogance, and being overbearing, hypercritical, or blatantly rude. These are not just unattractive qualities; they create serious personal, interpersonal, and societal problems.

(As I've said earlier, women, too, can exhibit traits of toxic masculinity, although they're more likely to be punished for such behavior than men are. Men can exhibit toxic femininity, too.)

We don't need unconscious men who are intolerant, abusive, and corruption. We need men who are conscious, men who shine, men who know that many of the myths they have been taught about men and women are false. The men who shine are powerful and kind, focused and creative. Warm-hearted and driven. Firm and tolerant. A strong man is a man who is conscious of all parts of himself, including his feminine energy. These conscious men who can help heal the wounds in humanity and build a more humane world. They are the "real men."

For us to get there, we need to understand the truth about male and female energies.

Masculine and feminine energy

Feminine energy is the energy of life. It's the energy of "being," not "doing" (which is associated with masculine energy). Bright traits of feminine energy include creativity, being in the flow, having fine intuition and expressing the nurturing others by listening, loving, openness, and empathy. The immature side of feminine energy can manifest as people-pleasing, not speaking up or being indecisive, submissive, or unfocused. Oprah Winfrey, Nelson Mandela, The Dalai Lama, Brené Brown, Bob Dylan, and Keanu Reeves manifest positive feminine energy.

Positive masculine energy is associated with action, focus, strength, mission, purpose, drive, achievement, power, logic, reason, directness, clarity, predictability, stability, thinking, task, and structure. The dark side of masculine energy manifests as being controlling, dismissive, overactive, coercive, and reckless. Examples of positive masculine energy include William Wallace (Mel Gibson's character in *Braveheart*), Muhammad Ali, Katniss Everdeen of *The Hunger Games*, Malala Yousafzai, Emmeline Pankhurst, and Florence Nightingale.

One is not more necessary or respectable than the other. Rather, they're complementary. Masculine energy needs to be in balance with feminine energy. Here's one example of how this works: Masculine energy has a task focus; it wants to get things done. Feminine energy is people-focused. Combine the two, and you have a person who gets things done and engages people in the process. Think of a leader you have admired. They likely did this very well.

Deconstructing the myths

We learn—or, more accurately, are brainwashed by—the norms of the society we are born into, inheriting whatever belief systems come with. Genetics can also shape our worldview. Current research in behavioral epigenetics indicates that past trauma—whether our own or that of our ancestors—leaves molecular scars that attach to our DNA. We inherit not only physical characteristics but also the behavioral and psychological tendencies of our ancestors. These myths are programmed into us and can only be unlearned with our conscious effort and participation.

Psychospiritual writer and spiritual mentor Aletheia Luna points out some common myths about men:

1. Men shouldn't cry.

2. Men must be stoic and not express their emotions.

3. Men must have a successful career.

4. Men must be the head of the household.

5. Men are primarily logical and left-brain oriented.

6. Men have to be interested in sports.

7. Men are the protectors of women and children.

8. Men must dominate women physically, sexually, and financially.

9. Men are expected to be aggressively self-confident.

10. Men must look strong and have muscles.

Here are some common myths about women:

Women are overly emotional.

Women who are aggressive are "bitchy."

Women should have sexy bodies.

Women are not good at sports.

Women are not funny.

Women aren't strong enough to be leaders.

Women must conform to ideal beauty standards.

Women are irrational.

Women are primarily illogical and right-brained.

Women cry easily.

Women talk too much.

These myths run deep and need to be confronted, called out, eliminated, and transformed.

I've discovered deep patterns in me about men and women. When I notice one or when someone else points one out, it's painful. I feel threatened, vulnerable, and sometimes helpless. How can I cleanse myself of these ingrained beliefs?

It is not easy work. Changing any belief begins by first noticing it. When we realize we believe in a myth, we can begin to let go of it. It's the ones we don't notice that hold us back. Who is most likely to expose the false beliefs men have about the masculine and feminine? Anyone who has already freed themselves from the myths.

Here are a few ways you can begin to deconstruct these myths:

- ¤ *Reread the lists above stating myths about men and women.* Very honestly, ask yourself which myths you believe. When you identify one—on the list or in life—ask yourself: Why do you think that? What work is necessary to change that belief?

- ¤ *Associate with people who are working on being more aware of their own limiting beliefs.* If you have any false beliefs, there's a good chance you will find out. In my experience, if you don't associate with women or men who will challenge you, your false beliefs will endure unchecked.

- ¤ *Associate with men who have a well-developed feminine side.* Look for men who have artistic, musical, or creative interests. They are very likely accessing their right brain, the more feminine and creative side of their personality. What can you learn from them?

- ¤ *When a myth surfaces, look at it closely.* What's its origin? The first place to look is within your family of origin and the society in which you grew up. Maybe it's in your DNA, too. What do you know about your ancestors? How did they live? What trauma, if any, did they experience? How might that be playing out in your life?

¤ *Reframe false beliefs.* For example, if you believe women are too sensitive, you might reframe it as: *One of the gifts of feminine energy is to be sensitive.* If you find yourself invested in the idea that all women are too sensitive, investigate your own sensitivity levels. Why is that a trigger for you? What negative associations do you have with sensitivity, and why?

¤ Stay vigilant. If you identify one myth, there are likely more.

Integration

If we're male, we need to tap into our inner feminine. That way, we can develop our ability to listen, nurture, empathize, feel, and trust our intuition. We need to invite feminine energy and women into our lives, our boardrooms, and our politics, rather than making it necessary that it push its way into those arenas. That is not a balanced approach: it would be asking femininity to be more masculine.

When we integrate masculine and feminine energy within ourselves, we can be powerful and compassionate, bold and kind, purposeful and caring, strong-willed and patient, demanding and collaborative. Feminine energy doesn't make us weak; it makes us stronger, smarter, and more effective—sexier, too.

To be successful professionally and personally, we need to understand and accept our feminine qualities and graciously love and invite into our world the beauty and gifts that feminine energy brings. And we need mature masculine energy that is honorable, forthright, and just.

How men can develop their feminine energy

If you find yourself getting angry, frustrated, too aggressive, overworked, scattered, or exhausted, you're likely running on too much masculine energy and not enough feminine, regardless of your gender. The following practices can help you get back in balance—they require feminine energy. Some are obvious, some not.

Make time for reflection. When we're too busy, we rarely give our brains time to rest, but brains need rest to function optimally. When we're too busy, we move from one thing to the next without a break. Try these:

- ¤ Take 15 minutes a day to sit quietly and let your mind wander.
- ¤ Journal for a few minutes in the morning.
- ¤ Take a nap.
- ¤ Go for a walk.

Practice meditation. When we connect to our Higher Self through meditation, we are directly accessing the source of feminine energy within us, our life force. A regular meditation practice opens the pathway to our hearts. The more we keep ourselves open, the more feminine energy flows.

Develop your intuition. Trust your feelings more. Start by paying attention to the subtle messages your body sends you. Notice when your stomach, chest, or throat feels tight. Notice when you feel relaxed. Observe what you are doing or thinking in each situation. What's the connection? Pause before making decisions. Look within for guidance. What does your gut tell you?

Be in nature. Nature is abundant with life and feminine energy. It's why we are attracted to forests, mountains, and oceans—they're restorative. We intuitively know that taking regular walks, hiking, and looking up at the stars are recharging.

Be creative. Creative energy is feminine energy. When we manifest an idea into reality, we are tapping into our feminine energy. Writing, painting, cooking, drawing, dancing, and playing music are expressions of feminine energy. So are things like putting together a presentation, developing plans, brainstorming, and developing new business ventures. When we immerse ourselves in creative activities, we enter into the flow of feminine energy. We experience the magic of creation. It energizes us and unleashes joy in our body and mind.

Build emotional capacity. Any work requiring high degrees of logic and rationality draws on masculine energy. Emotions flow from our feminine energy. Take a few minutes each day to notice how you feel. Start with how your body feels, then see how *you* feel. The more you do this, the more in touch you'll be with your feminine energy. If talking about your feelings is difficult, this process will gradually make it easier.

Enjoy the little things. The harder we work, the harder it is to disengage. We push on, and before we know it, we're not enjoying life as much as we could. Take time to savor the moment—read a few pages of your new book, take a warm bath and stretch out on your living room rug, or call a friend. These are the moments of luxury, brief minutes of enjoying the simple pleasures of life. You'll feel better and just a bit more relaxed when you enjoy the little things life offers.

Embrace transformation. Feminine energy isn't just about caring, nurturing, and creativity. It's also about letting go of the old and bringing in the new. Masculine energy is associated with stability and reliability. Feminine energy is the energy of change and transformation. If something isn't working for you any longer—a job or where you live—it may be time for a shift. Lean into the part of you seeking a new frontier, a fresh start. The old must go before the new comes in. Call on your feminine energy.

*   *   *

Bringing together opposite dimensions creates wholeness. When a man is balanced and whole, he can access his full power, behave like a gentleman, make the world a better place, and be stronger, smarter, and sexier, too. No bull.

Six Essential Practices to Live
a Satisfied Life

You'll find richness in a path of peace

As I've mentioned, I'm 70 now. I'm in the final third of my life, and I'm more aware than ever that the seconds and minutes are ticking away. So, more than ever before, I ask myself what's really important.

I don't experience a youthful sense of immortality anymore—the belief I can do almost anything and survive. Although I feel spiritually, mentally, physically, and emotionally strong, I feel vulnerable, too. I feel vulnerable because I know life is a gift. I feel blessed to still be here, especially when old friends suddenly die. It's not up to me when I go. The only thing up to me is how I choose to think and behave.

So, while I am still here, my goal is to live a peaceful life in alignment with my values. That goal is my North Star. Here are my six essential practices for staying true to that goal:

Define what's important to you and stick with it.

Whatever work I do now must be enjoyable, meaningful to me, and of service to others. If it doesn't meet those criteria, I don't do it. As a result, I say No to more things than ever before. I don't chase opportunities just because of the money; in fact, I don't chase anything. I let opportunities come to me by staying true to my values.

Things were different when I first entered the mainstream workforce at the age of 33. I worked in retail, selling women's shoes and men's shirts. My criteria for a job were not complicated—I needed someone to hire and pay me. Period. I didn't care if it was meaningful, enjoyable, or of service to others. Bills had to get paid. So I did what I had to do.

Sometimes, lousy jobs are the price we pay to learn what we like and what we don't like. Sure enough, within a few years, I found work I enjoyed, and it's pretty much been that way ever since. Define your values. Find what you like to do. Then, get good at it and stick to your values. Always.

Be kind and forgiving to yourself.

I've been tough on myself throughout life. Family of origin stuff was planted deep in my DNA. It's taken a lot of work to dig through the layers, reprogram my operating system, and exorcise most of my demons.

I've eased up on the negative self-talk, the perfectionism, and the impossible standards. Instead of denial, I've faced my flaws full-on, embracing them and doing what I can to make improvements. I still stumble, but now I catch myself sooner when I go off-track.

The less harsh I am with myself, the better I feel. Less guilt, shame, and embarrassment. More happiness. More peace. And—the best thing of all perhaps—the kinder and more loving I am to myself, the kinder and more loving I am to others.

Let go of guilt or remorse from the past.

Guilt is debilitating. Acceptance is energizing. If my mind tries to drag me into a discussion about what a terrible person I've been, I release those thoughts as quickly as possible. If not, they suck the energy right out of me. If I'm genuinely pursuing a peaceful life, this type of self-torture has no place. None at all.

Holding on to remorse is like carrying a giant stone on your back—you'll slowly get crushed. People who stand tall—literally and figuratively—don't carry the past. They've set it down. The more I make peace with the past, the lighter and brighter I am.

Be tolerant of others.

I've written plenty of articles about the differences between arrogance and humility. Tolerance is a direct manifestation of humility because the mindset of humility recognizes and respects the opinions and idiosyncrasies of others.

I have a lovely wife whom I adore. She's helped me heal wounds from the past and discover a new way of being. Before we met, I asked the Universe for a woman who could contain my sometimes out-of-control energy. The Universe listened and delivered.

She can undoubtedly contain me, and sometimes I don't like it. She'll do and say things I find perplexing. I'll think, "Well, that's not the way I would do it!" The egoic part of me wants her to be like me. My mind tries to convince me that if she is more like me, my problems with her behavior will go away.

Absolute lunacy.

I'll never find peace when I insist other people change. It's not my job to change their minds or behavior. My job is to accept what is. If she's doing something that bothers me, of course, I can make a reasonable request. "Please don't interrupt me when I'm speaking."

When it comes to someone's viewpoints, opinions, choices, and style, acceptance is wisdom and a step forward on the path to a peaceful life.

Appreciate what you have.

We often celebrate what we have, but too often, we judge ourselves by what we don't have. New job—celebrate. Birth of a child—celebrate. The ability to afford a vacation—celebrate. But the inner critic is also lurking beneath the surface, ready to tell us what we don't have. Unfortunately, the world doesn't help, either; it bombards us with messages about everything we don't have.

Case in point. The new iPhone 13 ads were everywhere, but I had a very usable iPhone when the 13 came out. I didn't need a new one, but the ads were after me, trying to convince me I did. They planted a seed in the back of my mind, reminding me that I didn't have the latest iPhone. But I wasn't biting. I was grateful to be alive, enjoying what I had. There was no need to get involved with what I didn't have.

Nurture your inner world.

There are two aspects of this: meditation and mindset. Meditation came first for me. It's given me a connection to my spirit. After 50 years of practicing, I enjoy a simple but profound experience of my life force on a daily basis. It's deeply fulfilling, grounding, and lights me up from the inside. So whatever your practice may be, please keep at it. The older you get, the more it's going to mean to you.

The mindset work started later in my life. If I had to do it over again, I'd begin in my 20s. Over the last 15 years, I've worked on clarifying my values and paying much more attention to my attitude and beliefs. My core values—humility, integrity, responsibility, and honesty—have been instrumental in helping me develop a more positive and vibrant mindset. I've watched false beliefs and limitations drop away, leaving me more open, curious, ambitious, and courageous.

The inner work never ends, and the time to do it is—well—I'd say all the time.

*   *   *

No matter who you are or what you have or don't have, the richness in life can be found by pursuing a peaceful life.

Ten Things You Don't Need in Your Life

Take a personal inventory and bin the garbage!

We accumulate many things throughout our lives—possessions, habits, thought patterns, and beliefs. So, while you can certainly add new skills, healthier choices, and better habits, it's also crucial to get rid of things you don't need.

With 70 years of life experience under my belt, here are my suggestions for the top 10 things you don't need to accumulate.

1. The approval of others

If you want to have a safe, predictable, be-like-everybody-else life, seek the approval of others—your parents, friends, work colleagues, and society at large. However, if you want to blaze your own trail and live a life of exploration, adventure, and learning, then get off the beaten path and listen to the voices that are telling you to go for what you want.

You don't need anyone's approval. You've got everything you need right inside you. So tap into it and hold your head high.

2. Believing you're smarter than you are

If you think you're smarter than you are, then you've got an inflated opinion of yourself. The problem with that isn't that you think you know more than everybody else; it's that you believe you're right and everyone else is either stupid or wrong. This is arrogance, and it's deadly.

If you fall into this trap, you will criticize anyone who disagrees with you and label them a loser, an idiot, or a menace to society. Arrogance creates separation and animosity.

Ditch arrogance for curiosity. Be brilliant. Have your own beliefs and opinions but realize that not everyone sees the world the way you do.

3. Passivity

Not having an opinion, not speaking up, giving hints but not asking for what you want, or letting people take advantage of your good nature will not help you find peace, happiness, or success. These unproductive behaviors exist because a part of you has become disenfranchised. Find that part. Heal it, love it, and bring it home.

The real you is powerful and confident. Being passive is a choice. Do what it takes to build your inner warrior and let it step forward, express an opinion, speak up for what you want, draw boundaries, and stand tall.

4. Avoiding responsibility

Blaming others and cursing your circumstances are synonymous with avoiding responsibility. When you don't take ownership of what you create, you're making a dirty deal with the devil. The devil says, "I can get you off the hook and make you feel innocent and blameless. All you have to do is give me your power."

But when you relinquish your power, you become weak, resentful, and eventually bitter. You become *power-full* by fully accepting responsibility for what you do and say. After all, you have control over your choices and behavior. They're all yours. They don't belong to anyone else.

The next time you're involved in an argument, stop and ask yourself, "What's my contribution to this situation?" Then, use the answer as a way to begin a resolution conversation.

5. Playing it safe

If you're staying in your comfort zone and avoiding being challenged, you aren't growing or learning. And when you stop learning, you become stale, brittle, and fragile. I know it sounds harsh, but it's true.

Learning and challenging yourself will keep you agile, flexible, and nimble. You'll feel more vibrant, and you can accomplish much more than you think.

I once took a calculated risk leaving the security of a cushy corporate job and joining a fledgling start-up. Three years later, it crashed and almost burned. Yet, I walked away rich with knowledge, skills, and experience that transformed my life.

We need the right amount of challenge to grow, learn, and find out who we are. You can't do that by playing it safe—but you can by taking carefully examined risks.

6. Being reckless

The other side of playing it safe is being reckless—doing things that can harm you or others. Being reckless typically involves extreme behavior, addiction, and selfishness. Unresolved psychological issues are usually behind reckless behavior. I've been reckless, and when it caught up with me, I had to dig deep and face the music. It wasn't pretty, but I turned my life around, and it blossomed like never before.

Extremist tendencies are a blessing and a curse. Lots of talent, creativity, and smarts are incredible gifts—but they have to be managed and channeled towards goodness and service to others. Left unchecked, they can develop into recklessness.

7. Being small-minded

Being small-minded includes judging others, making assumptions, being overly critical, and being slow to forgive. We fall into small-mindedness when we lack curiosity, live in fear, and feel at risk. We've forgotten and have become disconnected from an essential part of ourselves—our heart.

Being small-minded exists in the absence of fulfillment. The way out of being small-minded is to find out what is lacking in your life. Is it a connection with yourself or with others? Is it not knowing what you want? Is it the lack of meaningful work? Is it being stuck in limiting beliefs? When you are connected to your heart and experiencing inner peace, it's impossible to be small-minded.

8. Living beyond your means

Living beyond your means is recklessness disguised as living in the moment. I'm talking about racking up debt, maxing out your credit cards, and doing things like renting an apartment or leasing a car you really can't afford. I know people that made plenty of money during their career, and now, at retirement age, they can't afford to stop working.

I also know people who had moderately paying jobs and retired with a million bucks in the bank. They lived within their means and invested wisely. Unless you are loaded, you do not want to be paying a giant mortgage or a big rent payment when you're 65 years old. You want to have the lowest overhead possible so you can have the freedom to do whatever you choose. If you're still carrying significant financial obligations, you'll feel the pinch to the day you die.

Live within your means now so you're not caught with your pants down later on.

9. Not paying enough attention to your health

Poor health equals a poor quality of life. Mental, emotional, spiritual, and physical health are all important, and all require effort. It's easy to focus on just one or two and ignore the others, but they're really like four legs on a stool. If one leg is weak, it affects the entire system, creating imbalance. From time to time, take an inventory and ask yourself:

- ¤ *What thought patterns do I notice? What beliefs are helping or hindering me?* (Mental)

- ¤ *How am I feeling? What emotions keep showing up? Am I content most of the time or not?* (Emotional)

- ¤ *What am I doing to nurture myself regularly? Do I feel a connection to my inner being? Do I know what I stand for?* (Spiritual)

- ¤ *What's happening in my body? What do I notice? Am I getting enough daily exercise? Am I eating as healthily as I can? What can I do more of? Less of?* (Physical)

You want to be sharp, active, happy, and fit when you get older, so take care of your health now.

10.   Being attached to limiting beliefs

We all have beliefs about ourselves. Some are healthy, and some are not. Unhealthy beliefs are those that keep you playing small. If you can identify them and let them go, new doors can open.

One of the most important principles I've learned is: The way we think—our attitude and mindset, otherwise known as our being—drives our behavior (what we do), which generates our results (what we have). Be-Do-Have.

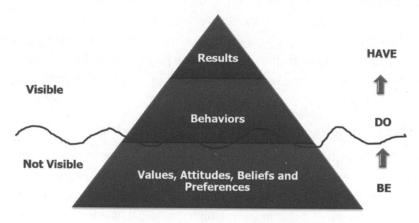

Being more effective, happy, and fulfilled isn't achieved by focusing on your results or even on your behavior. It's accomplished by looking at your inner world—your being—and making the necessary adjustments to your mindsets, attitudes, and beliefs. Keep your inside world clean, be as conscious as you be, and the results will come.

*   *   *

Without these 10 things, you'll not only be just fine, you'll thrive.

PART 5

Meditation
and Spirituality

Five Things I've Learned from 49 Years of Meditation

Looking up reminds us to look within

I looked up at the stars on a clear night recently, and the beauty of our universe was undeniable. Seeing the vast cosmos—of which we are just a tiny part—put my life in perspective. I felt peaceful and blessed to be alive and humble. I thought, *"Looking up is good for us."* So is looking within. Meditation.

1. The purpose of meditation

The purpose of meditation is not to control your mind, hear your inner voice, improve your health, find your passion in life, or solve your problems. Some of those may happen in the process of meditating, but they're not the purpose of this practice. Imagine someone told you that there was buried treasure in your backyard. You start digging day after day, enjoying the exercise and fresh air. You notice you are getting stronger and feeling better, but you still haven't gotten to the treasure. While there are benefits to digging, the purpose of digging is to find the treasure. And the purpose of meditation is to connect to your inner self and experience joy, peace, and happiness. We need not forget there is buried treasure within us.

So, let's put the word "meditation" aside for a moment. "Meditation" can mean many things, so let's switch it up. Let's use "going within."

Go back a few thousand years before modern religion. Our ancient ancestors were connected to the earth, the elements, and the changing of the seasons. They celebrated the cycles of the moon and the sun and established rituals to mark their importance. If our ancestors wanted to go within, they would seek a shaman, a teacher, a wise man or woman, or a guru. In Sanskrit, "guru" means "dispeller of darkness." Gurus were teachers that dispelled the darkness and revealed light—the inner light. I bet the ancients weren't worried about finding their passion and controlling their overactive minds. They wanted to connect to their souls.

1. We are designed to go within

The techniques of going within are ancient, and they're simple. We pay attention to our outer world through our senses. We don't have to make much effort to see, hear, and feel what's around us. In the same way, it's natural to turn our attention inward. Instead of looking, hearing, and feeling our outer world, we invert those capabilities to discover what lies within us. Going within is not dependent on intelligence or physical attributes such as a healthy, fully functioning body.

The process of going within is natural and easy once you learn a few basic principles. No books or instruction manuals are necessary.

2. The experience of meditation is something you feel

I've been going within for over 49 years. I can tell you there is plenty of joy and happiness inside. My experience and the experience of many others I know is that the experience one has through meditation is not a belief or something to be imagined. It's as real as eating a delicious meal. For example, if you were very hungry and went to a restaurant, read the menu, ordered, and ate a great meal, are you going to tell your friends about how great it was to read the menu and order the food? Heck no. You're going to talk about how good the food was because eating the food was the purpose of going to the restaurant. You experienced the purpose. Ultimately, the purpose of going within is to experience inner peace and contentment.

3. Thirst for the inner experience helps sustain the practice of meditation

Imagine it's a hot day and you're outside for hours without water. Your throat is dry; your body is crying out for water. You can't wait for your thirst to be quenched. You know you need water. Nothing else will satisfy you. Even the *idea* of anything else is unthinkable. Someone offers you a glass of cold water, so you gulp it down, quenching your thirst.

The same principle applies to going within. Because inner fulfillment feels good, you want more of it. So, the practice of meditation is not a chore, something you force yourself to do. When you are thirsty for inner peace, you're naturally drawn to it. You want to experience the joy of drinking the water that quenches your inner thirst.

4. The breath helps us go within

Our minds are very active—incessantly replaying the past and worrying about or anticipating the future. Thankfully, as meditators, our job is not to control our minds. Our job is to go within and do nothing—just be the observer and gently bring our attention to the breath. In doing so, the mind naturally slows down as our connection to our spirit grows.

The breath is neither in the past nor the future. On the other hand, the thinking mind—the ego—lives in the past or the future. It doesn't inhabit the present because it is not pure consciousness. Many forms of meditation suggest placing one's attention on one's breath because the breath is always in the present. It can hook the mind and soothe it. The experience we want when going within is just behind the breath. It's there, quietly waiting for us not to overlook it. When the thinking mind dissolves, the inner experience of consciousness, light, and energy appears.

It takes time and practice, but believe me, it's well worth it. We are part of a universe that reflects what is within us. When you look up at the stars on a clear night and see that unbelievable mass of swirling galaxies, stars, and planets twinkling at you, what you see, in its unique way, is inside you, too.

Looking up at the stars puts life in perspective. When you connect to it, you'll experience real happiness arising within you. You'll realize that the experience of true joy is not derived from people, places, or things. It comes from the soul, and the soul is naturally happy.

*   *   *

Meditation has helped me become a better person, parent, and husband. It's helped me realize that my true happiness doesn't come from people, places, and things. It comes from within me. And what I've found in there is truly a blessing. I hope you find it, too.

Five Ways to Fire Up
Your Meditation Practice

Easy steps to keep at it when the world gets in the way

I've been practicing raja yoga (royal union) meditation for a long time— 49 years, to be exact. It's an essential part of my life, and it's helped me become more patient, kind, curious, happy, and fulfilled. Every day, I realize I have more to learn. In fact, I often feel like I'm merrily stumbling my way along, tripping over what I thought I had already learned. But I've come to accept that this is the way the journey is—I'll always be evolving, learning, growing, and stumbling.

I practice meditation because I know there is inner fulfillment within me—the place described in every scripture throughout the existence of humankind. And I also know that it's one of the most practical beneficial things anyone can do for their well-being.

We are physical, mental, emotional, and spiritual beings. We need to be in balance in all areas to have overall well-being. Hectic, drama-filled lives can debilitate us and create imbalance. Meditation helps bring us into equilibrium so that all parts of us work together harmoniously.

Here are five things to keep in mind that have helped me keep at it over the years:

1. Be thirsty

My journey into meditation started with the thought that there must be a life force in the Universe. Something must be sustaining all this, something that can be experienced. I learned in high school chemistry that all matter is energy, some moving quickly, some moving very slowly—protons, neutrons, subatomic particles, quarks—always invisibly vibrating. I thought: *Energy has to be within me, too, doesn't it?* When I learned there was a way to go within and experience that energy, I wanted to know more. I was thirsty to know what was within me, sustaining me. That thirst was my motivation to learn to meditate, and it has been the main reason I have stuck with it.

Over the years, I've learned that the keys for me to stay committed to a goal are to practice regularly, remove drama from my life, and cultivate a curious mind. When we lose enthusiasm for what we are pursuing we lose our way. There have been times when I got caught up in giving more attention to things around me than within me. It's easy to forget that real, lasting satisfaction comes from our inner connection, not from people, places, and things. It's like discovering a new restaurant serving up fantastic food. Once you've been there, you want to go back because it was so good. It's the same with meditation. When we realize there is something there, we want to return to it; we want to have more.

2. Breathe properly

Martial arts, athletics, yoga, and meditation all speak to the importance of proper breathwork. For any meditation that involves breath, the deep and slow inhaling through the nose, helps the body settle into a still and quiet place. Breathing through the nose enables more control over your breathing and is healthier as the nose acts as a filter.

If you aren't sure if your breathing is deep, here is an exercise that can help. Sit down. Place one hand over your navel and the other hand on your sternum. Now breathe normally. If the hand on your navel moves, you are breathing deeply. This is called diaphragmatic breathing. If the other one moves, you are breathing more shallowly. When our breathing is shallow, we get less oxygen, which is less healthy for our body and our brain.

You can also check out your speaking voice. Is it coming from deep in your belly or your throat when you speak? If it's from the throat, your breathing is likely more shallow. If you feel it coming from your stomach, you're breathing deeply. Deep breathing, unlike shallow breathing, provides more oxygen to your lungs, and more oxygen is simply healthier for your body. Watch a sleeping baby breathe.

They breathe from their belly, filling up their little lungs with plenty of oxygen.

To help you focus on the breath, you can listen to the sound your breath makes as your lungs fill slowly and your diaphragm rises. The sound yogis have used for thousands of years is "So Hum." Try it while you breathe in through your nose. As you inhale, hear what sounds like "So." On the exhale, hear the sound "Hum." If you like, you can silently repeat So Hum as a mantra. Eventually, as you go deeper, you will forget about repeating the mantra. Your lungs are filling slowly like a balloon and then emptying. Just observe; no need to judge your progress. There is nothing to do.

Having a satisfying inner experience can take time if you are new to meditation. If you feel impatient with your progress, remember that correct breathing alone has enormous health benefits. Journalist James Nestor says in his new book, *Breath: The New Science of a Lost Art,* "Breathing properly can allow us to live longer and healthier lives. Breathing poorly, by contrast, can exacerbate and sometimes cause a laundry list of chronic diseases: asthma, anxiety, attention deficit hyperactivity disorder, hypertension, and more." With practice, our breathing will soften and our focus will drift to a place behind the breath, and that is where the experience of our inner self begins.

The mind needs something to focus on for it to settle down. When we are healthy, our breath is available to us all the time, and the mind can attach itself to the breath. Keep at it, and you'll be on your way to reaping the benefits of breathwork in no time.

3. Get comfortable

As you practice, you want to be comfortable, but not so comfortable that you fall asleep. If you aren't comfortable, it's tough to concentrate, and any aches and pains you have can be distractions. Yoga was developed over 4,000 years ago to prepare the body for meditation, so getting into a position where you can forget about your body is essential. I've been doing Hatha yoga regularly for the past few years, and it has considerably improved my ability to sit with ease. If you discover you have a bad case of head-bobbing, you're tired, and your body is telling you something. If you do fall asleep, just accept it—sleep!

I like to sit erect with my spine straight. I close my eyes and bring my attention inside to my breath. I am typically aware of my body as I begin my practice. I feel my lungs filling with air, rising and then falling, and I am aware of my body. My breath slows down, and my attention continues to be within, just observing and feeling the subtle energy that is there. Thoughts come and go. And if I wander off, I bring my awareness back to my breath. Before I know it, 15 or 20 minutes have passed.

4. Manage resistance

There may be times when just the thought of sitting down to meditate becomes unbearable. Or you might find that you've woken up late one morning and only have five minutes instead of 20 to do your practice. These things will happen, but it's important to keep focused and not let any resistance build up. If you wake up late and have only five minutes, use the time you have or do more later. And if you find that the thought of sitting down impossible, try and let go of any negative self-judgment. On the rare occasion when I find myself in this mode of thought—wanting to do anything but sit—I try to let go of any negative self-judgment. I say a prayer of gratitude or set an intention for the day: I'm going to have a day filled with success, abundance, and kindness, or I fully accept and trust the Universe in all that happens today.

Times when your mind is overactive can be challenging, too, so much that it's impossible to focus. Battling it is pointless. There is no value in trying to prove to yourself that you can conquer the mind and bring it to stillness. Just accept what is happening. You've tried. Remember, let go of any self-judgment. It's an opportunity to surrender and realize that you don't have control over your mind, and it's a poignant reminder that we aren't in control of anything.

Regardless of what happens, I do my best to be aware of my breath throughout the day, taking advantage of sitting in a meeting, waiting in line, or walking. If you find that resistance keeps returning, tell yourself: I can find 10 minutes every day for me to be with myself, in silence, in meditation. Tony Robbins famously said, "If you don't have 10 f***ing minutes for your life, you don't have a life."

5. Have an open heart

Having an inner experience of joy and fulfillment is a gift. When I open my eyes after practicing, I feel like I'm looking out from a sacred sanctuary where there is no conflict, no chaos, no hate, or selfishness. I don't have to be someone; I don't have to perform; I don't have to compete or struggle. I'm safe and accepted for who I am here, with all my flaws and weaknesses. No one is judging me here; this is where I learn not to judge others.

This sanctuary is incredible. I can't create it, I can't summon it, I can't govern it, nor do I own it. It appears when it so desires, blessing me with its wisdom. I'm the receiver. It asks for very little from me. It merely says: Just look within, approach me with an open heart and mind, and make a small effort to let go and trust.

In her book, *Mindset: The New Psychology of Success*, psychologist Carol Dweck describes an open mind as a growth mindset. Interestingly, the characteristics of a grown mindset support a meditation practice:

¤ Embraces challenges
¤ Persists in the face of setbacks
¤ Sees effort as a path to mastery
¤ Learns from criticism
¤ Finds lessons and inspiration in the success of others

*   *   *

I approach my meditation practice like I'm going on an adventure. I have no idea what will happen. I just need to show up and be ready to receive whatever comes.

How To Reduce the Noise in
Your Head Before You Meditate

A clear psyche can improve your inner experience

Meditation is challenging enough, even when you're having a good day. If you're stressed out, worried, or dealing with an overactive mind, it just simply makes things more difficult. Ideally, the more you can manage your mental clutter before you meditate, the better.

For example, I woke up at 2:00 a.m. recently because I was worrying about something that might happen in the future. I got agitated for a while, then took a few deep breaths and said to myself, several times, "You've done everything you can to deal with this problem. The Universe has your back. Just let go."

I focused on my breathing and gazed into the soft light starting to swirl in my third eye. Acceptance and calm replaced tension. I soon fell back to sleep.

I need to be more careful about what I let into my consciousness—negative thoughts, doubts, fears, and false stories. With all the crazy stuff going on, an inner place of tranquility and calm is a welcome relief and reminder of life's deeper purpose—to experience joy and appreciate being alive.

The cleaner your psyche is, the easier it is to experience inner calm. A clean psyche means less chatter, less agitation. Conversely, a cluttered psyche full of noise, frustration, and annoyance makes meditation, as well as everyday living, more difficult.

Here are five things that can clutter up your psyche, along with my suggestions for dealing with each one.

1. Don't worry about things you can't control

It's the nature of the active mind to think about the past and ponder the future. However, it's not helpful when thinking about the future turns into worrying about it—making up worst-case scenarios, believing, and acting on them. Worry takes us out of the present moment and creates tension. Tension creates anxiety, and anxiety makes meditation more difficult.

When we focus on what isn't within our control, we suffer. What can you do instead? Notice when you are worrying. In his book, *The Power of Now*, Eckhardt Tolle suggests asking yourself, "Is there joy, ease, and lightness in what I am doing? If there isn't, then time is covering up the present moment and life is perceived as a burden or struggle." He explains that when we live in and honor the present moment, unhappiness and struggle melt away. The key to getting into the "now" is to notice where you are putting your attention.

When we meditate, we let future-related thoughts drift by and release attachment to them. Smile at them and say, "Thanks very much for the concern," and let them go. Do what is within your control, and then accept your situation as it is.

2. Don't rehash breakdowns

Close relationships can bring shadow elements within us to the surface. For example, even though my wife and I are both long-time, regular meditators and love each other to bits, we still occasionally lock heads over ridiculous day-to-day issues.

The other day, we disagreed because I thought something so obvious would be the same for her. I got hooked, raised my voice, and passionately stated my point of view. That's about the worst thing I could have done because she merely met my fire with a strong pushback in my face.

We dropped the conversation since I had to leave for an appointment, but the residue of friction was in the back of my mind for the next four hours, following me around like a hooded stranger from a creepy horror movie. If I sat down to meditate during that time, I'd be dealing with multiple voices arguing who did what and who's to blame. Not a conducive environment for experiencing inner peace.

When I got home later that evening, we agreed to have a heart-based conversation. I apologized for making an assumption, and we swiftly resolved the matter. I felt the agitation leave my psyche. Clean again.

The essential thing in my marriage is connection. If one of us doesn't feel it, we do our best to raise the issue. We make time for five to 10 minutes of heart-based conversation every day, which means we stop everything and say what we are grateful for about each other and about our lives.

If you feel agitated with someone or incomplete after an interaction, don't ignore it. When you're ready, ask to have a completion conversation. Find your way back to equilibrium.

3. Face the undiscussables

I call those things that we don't speak to someone about—even though we know they need to be addressed—"undiscussables." Undiscussables are like large files on your computer; they take up lots of space and consume a lot of psychic energy. You know what's it like when disk space gets full—your computer is sluggish and runs slowly. If it were human, you would say it was having a bad day.

When you have many unresolved issues, they can interfere with your ability to find inner peace because they're constantly running in the background, adding clutter to your psyche, encouraging shadow behavior, and draining your power.

What can you do? Face the undiscussables.

It takes courage to face what you don't want to confront. But unfortunately, false beliefs often prevent us from having conversations that can clean our psyche and set us free. For example, five years ago, I was in a marriage that wasn't serving me, afraid to have a conversation about ending it because of the hardships I imagined would occur due to divorce. None of it turned out to be true. In fact, having that ending conversation transformed my entire life because I cleaned up the undiscussable and rediscovered my power.

Undiscussables need careful consideration. Some might be too hot to touch for reasons only you know. Others might exist because they've been ignored and brushed off as "too much work right now." You think, "I'll deal with it later." But those are the ones that deserve a second look; they might very well be worth the work. If you know they're holding you back from reaching your full potential, they deserve to be dealt with.

If you have an undiscussable you're harboring, ask yourself what you're afraid of. Write down your fears. I bet they are future-imagined, worst-case scenarios. You won't have enough money. Someone will get angry with you. You'll be left all alone.

Think carefully about those fears, perhaps work with a life coach, and figure out how to turn this unmentionable subject into a frank, loving, and respectful conversation. What you think will be a disaster on the other side of the undiscussable might just be the life you always dreamed of.

4. Don't live in fear

Fear is like a virus; it needs a host—and that is us. Think of fear as an outsider, a thief trying to find a way into your home. Fear is not a natural state of mind like love, peace, and tranquility. Fear peers into the windows of our minds looking for an entry point—a vulnerability, a doubt, a sensitive weakness, or an old wound. It attaches itself when it finds one and begins an insidious campaign to enroll us in a fear-based paradigm. Small fears that are tolerated can turn into a pervasive, fearful state of mind. Fear invites dis-ease.

Fear is optional, like a side of onion rings with your burger. It's not part of the main meal. Fear holds us back, keeps us locked up in the smaller version of who we are. What can you do instead? Notice and get rid of fear-based thinking. Just as darkness cannot exist in the presence of light, fear cannot exist in the presence of love, faith, and trust. Guard against fear by being vigilant, observing your thoughts without judgment, and carefully choosing which ones to believe.

Fear often manifests as tension within the body. If you notice any part of your body tightening, your gut, chest, or shoulders, check what you are thinking. If you spot a fear-based thought pattern, you'll probably find you're worrying about something that hasn't happened yet. Do your best to let it go.

Lately, I've been using the affirmations, "I'm well taken care of. I have nothing to worry about. The Universe has my back." As soon as I move my attention away from any drama-filled story in my head and invite in trust and faith, I feel my body and mind relax. Where we put our attention makes all the difference. We get to choose what thoughts we entertain. Choose the good ones.

5. Don't behave badly and do nothing to change it

We know when we're cutting corners, telling white lies, and playing games we shouldn't be playing. They consume energy that could be used for more productive purposes. When I've been way out of alignment with my highest values, I couldn't tap into my full capabilities. As a result, I was more frequently ill or suffered physical injuries. We often think injuries have nothing to do with our mental and spiritual health. Much of the time, they are directly related.

We all have our bad days and know what it's like to act like a jerk. Acting like one doesn't originate in our hearts; it comes from ego and arrogance. Misbehaving is easy; it takes no effort, just like judging others. Denying being a jerk is the real problem because denial is like laying wet cement between us and our ego—when it dries, we're even more identified with our ego.

The whole point of meditation is to create separation from our ego and connection to our true self, so anything that provides more energy to the ego is counterproductive and will inhibit a more profound meditation experience.

What can you do instead? Call out your own bullshit.

I'm not saying this is easy to do, but it's an essential practice if you're serious about spiritual growth. Admitting you're wrong takes guts because your ego will take a beating. But if you're after the primo experience of life, you'll have to get used to giving your ego a kick in the ass. In the beginning, it hurts more, but as you continue, you'll learn to accept your failings as invitations to further learning and enlightenment. I'm not saying it's Happy-Days-Are-Here-Again time, but it's a sure sign you're on the road to accepting your humanness.

But here is the twist: admit when you've screwed up without punishing yourself. If I continually berate myself for not being enlightened enough or for not being the perfect companion, I merely create an endless loop of suffering. First, I misbehave, then punish myself for doing so, and before you know it, I'll treat others the same way. When they make a mistake, I'll happily shame them, and so on.

Take ownership when you screw up. Accept your imperfections. Be kind to yourself and others. This mindset will help bring your psyche into a more tranquil state and make meditation that much easier.

*   *   *

Meditation can soothe an active mind, but it's not a miracle pill, either. It doesn't fix us, and it's not meant to heal all our troubles. Meditation is a gentle but firm lover. Approach her with care.

The more we keep our psyche clean, the easier it is to show up for our meditation practice with a humble mind and an open heart, ready to receive what is given.

Healthy Relationships
Begin with Finding Peace Within

Meditation can help you locate your truest self

There is nothing better than being in a loving, peaceful relationship with your spouse or partner—and nothing worse than being stuck in a relationship prone to tension and contempt. To have the former—in other words, to build a great relationship with someone else—you first need to have a healthy relationship with yourself.

Imagine you've just finished a wonderful meal and are relaxing by candlelight in your favorite spot, enjoying a piece of chocolate with your partner. It feels so good you almost don't notice it. You experience an absence of wanting anything else. You feel whole without the need for more. This is fulfillment—and it exists within us all the time.

Meditation can help bring us into an experience of fulfillment in a world where we're led to believe that happiness and fulfillment are the results of worldly achievements. But when we live our lives believing that, we open the door to needless disappointment and suffering.

The two selves within:
the talkative mind and the silent mind

We seem to have two selves within us: our talkative mind, or ego, and our more natural self, the silent mind. Tim Gallwey, the author of the groundbreaking sports psychology book, *The Inner Game of Tennis*, refers to these two parts of ourselves as Self 1—our talkative mind—and Self 2, our more intuitive subconscious self—our silent mind.

When we believe the endless stream of thoughts, ideas, opinions, judgments, and negative self-talk of our over-active mind, we can develop limiting beliefs that inhibit us from being more fulfilled and happy.

But beneath the talkative mind is the silent mind—a place of intuition, feeling, intelligence, heart, and spirit; it is our life source, our consciousness. When we tap into the silent mind, we discover our true essence, which enables us to bring the treasures of peace, gratitude, love, and joy into our lives. The silent mind is our core, where we can experience inner contentment. Meditation helps us embrace the silent mind.

When I learned to meditate many years ago, I discovered a quiet, expansive place—a part of me I didn't realize existed beneath the talkative mind—that was full of joy and peace. I became the observer of my thoughts instead of just being lost in them. I could more clearly see my ego for what it was because I found something to identify with that was not my ego. It's like climbing a familiar mountain and discovering a path leading to a new peak. When you arrive at the new peak, you look over and see the summit where you've been before, but it looks different because you are apart from it.

In meditation, we experience our life force, where the ego and its agenda cannot exist. Consistently experiencing our inner self enables us to live our lives more freely. We can exist in loving relationships and enjoy them without believing they are the only source of our happiness, as mentioned at the top of this writing. A fulfilling relationship flows from the generosity, fulfillment, and love within us.

When we meditate, we access that part of ourselves that is full of love, and we can bring that positive energy into our relationships. We display our inner world through our words and actions. We don't say cruel things when we feel full of love, and, on the flip side, we struggle to be kind and generous when we feel resentful. We either nurture our relationships, or we destroy them by what we do and what we say. How we think and feel creates our words, behavior, and relationships. To change the nature of our relationship, we have to change our inner world.

The more we connect to our Higher Self, the more we can bring love and kindness to our relationships. We stop seeing them as a simple give and take: "I will do this for you if you do this for me." Instead, we see our relationships as an opportunity to give, grow, and learn how we can be better humans.

To change the nature of our relationships, we have to change our inner world.

Mariclaire and I each have a daily spiritual practice, but we still experience friction and arguments. Most of them are about being "right," resurfacing old wounds, or conflicting expectations and communication breakdowns. The friction never arises from too much kindness; it comes from the rubbish that bubbles up from the ego.

Most argument triggers are unconscious; they leak out from the ego and its unresolved issues. They surface through expressions of annoyance, judgment, selfishness, and criticism. The next time you face a complicated relationship issue, ask yourself, "What would love do?" In relationships, we can choose what to discourage and what to encourage.

In our relationship, Mariclaire and I discourage the following actions:

> Complaining about other people
>
> Focusing on what we can't control
>
> Replaying negative stories from the day: "I can't believe they did this!"
>
> Not taking responsibility
>
> Projecting on the other
>
> Letting disagreements linger
>
> Not communicating our expectations

And we encourage the following behavior:

Giving space to each other for quiet reflection and
meditation

Laughing at ourselves

Respecting personal boundaries

Resolving breakdowns quickly and owning our part

Revisiting our values and shared vision regularly

Sacred sex, music, dance, and creativity

Honoring nature and the rhythm of life through ceremony

Seeing the Divine in each other

Respect for our bodies and what we consume

Understanding the mind-body connection

Calling each other out on any bullshit

*　*　*

Embracing our silent minds through meditation helps us remember
that fulfillment is always within us. And when we are fulfilled with
ourselves, that fulfillment—and the love and joy that goes along
with it—manifests in our relationships. That's when beautiful things
happen.

The Power and Beauty of Meditation

To develop more patience, humility,
acceptance, and gratitude

"I'm living in fear of the future."

I winced when I read those words, written by an old friend dealing with grief over a marriage breakup and a fractured relationship with his son. I wanted to reach across the ocean and hug him. Fear is often about the worst-case future we can imagine: believing the current discomfort will never end.

We absorb what we put our attention on. If you focus on negativity, you'll become negative. Seek positive influence and inspiration, and you'll be inspired. When we practice meditation, we place our attention on perhaps the most potent, positive energy available to us—our life energy.

This life-sustaining force is a spiritual battery charger full of inspiration, clarity, and love. When we hook up to it, we not only experience the beauty of our inner world, but we absorb the essential qualities of that energy—patience, acceptance, humility, compassion, gratitude, and love. Beginning meditators often say they don't experience much at all. I've said that, too. However, I've learned to keep practicing, no matter what, because I know I'm developing invaluable qualities regardless of whether I merge into the ocean of bliss or not.

We call meditation "practice" because we are practicing—we're strengthening our character as we learn how to experience the majesty of our inner world. I don't think my friend is alone. There's a lot of fear, stress, and anxiety in the collective system right now; there's no better time to practice meditation.

Meditation raises our level of consciousness

David R. Hawkins, MD, PhD, an internationally renowned psychiatrist, physician, researcher, spiritual teacher, and author of many books, developed what he calls "scales of consciousness."

According to Hawkins' research, our levels of consciousness vibrate at unique frequencies and equate to different emotions, behaviors, and perspectives on life. For example, fear, which is a lower frequency state of consciousness, often manifests as anxiety. Fear makes us feel heavy and lethargic—as if we are carrying a burden, which we are. When we are depressed, our energy is low. It's difficult to smile or feel generous and enthusiastic about life. It's not uncommon for us to hunker down and literally disappear from view when we're struggling.

On the other hand, acceptance, which vibrates at a higher frequency, manifests emotionally as calmness, peace, and forgiveness. We feel lighter, energetic, and joyful when we live in a state of acceptance. Big difference. Meditation can raise our level of consciousness because we are focusing on the energy responsible for peace, joy, love, reason, acceptance, willingness, neutrality, and courage, elements of the flow state. It can help us shift our energy from "getting by" or "suffering" to higher levels of consciousness.

Meditation and acceptance

One of the most powerful things I've learned from practicing meditation for 49 years is the art of cultivating acceptance of what happens. Accepting what I can't control. Accepting a different point of view. Accepting what I experience in my meditation practice.

A quick personal story. If my wife hears me whining about something I can't change, she looks at me lovingly and says, "Aren't you the guy that writes about being more conscious?" "Yes, I am," I respond, "and I'm on the journey, too, just like everyone else, darling!" She laughs and says I ought to read my articles. I laugh and say I wrote them. She laughs and says, "Well, try doing what you write about!"

Acceptance is easier said than done sometimes, and sometimes we need time to pass through whatever we need to learn. Meditation is a great teacher for me because even though I make an effort to practice regularly and focus on my techniques, the inner experience is not something I can regulate, demand, or expect. The inner experience is a gift, and I have to approach the giver with an open heart, no expectations, and accept what is given.

There have been times for me when, after many hours of meditation, the experience seemed minimal, considering the effort I put in. So much time invested, with seemingly so little return. Or was there a return? There's always a return, but we might not notice immediately. Meditation practice is a lifelong journey, not a quick fix. Patience is required.

Acceptance and humility

As for my friend who's living in fear of the future: While he might not be able to change his circumstances, he can shift his perspective by looking through the lens of acceptance instead of fear. Acceptance, a stage of a high level of consciousness in the flow state, is an antidote to fear that can help bring us into the present moment. The present moment is where we can find peace; for the past or the future we can't do that. Acceptance holds hands with humility.

The attitudes of acceptance and humility help us realize we don't control everything—the world does not revolve around us. By living with a mindset of acceptance and humility, we understand that there is more than one way to view the world and that our opinion is one of many possible opinions. Acceptance and humility grant us the freedom to move on and not be attached to something we can't have. Acceptance keeps us in the present moment and frees us from regret and living in the past. Acceptance brings us into the now, into a higher vibration. Meditation fosters acceptance.

It's time to bring in Rumi, the 13th-century Persian mystic poet:

This being human is a guest house. Every morning a new arrival.
A joy, a depression, a meanness, some momentary awareness comes
as an unexpected visitor. Welcome and entertain them all! Even if
they are a crowd of sorrows, who violently sweep your house empty
of its furniture, still, treat each guest honorably. He may be clear-
ing you out for some new delight. The dark thought, the shame,
the malice. Meet them at the door laughing and invite them in.
Be grateful for whatever comes. Because each has been sent as a
guide from beyond.   —RUMI

So beautiful. Acceptance of what shows up in life—not resistance.
To be grateful for whatever comes: Rumi has set the bar high.

I have much to learn.

It's easy to overlook the infinite energy source within us because
it's subtle. It's vibrating at a very high frequency, but we can tune
into it. We can turn the dials and direct our attention inwards. It's
possible. We're designed for it. When we tap into that vast pool of
consciousness, there are no thoughts, there is no time, there's just
pure energy. We become the observer, and when we merge with
the Universal Consciousness, we enter a unique place within. Our
breathing slows. Thoughts appear and swiftly leave as we continue
to do nothing but experience the moment. And then there are those
moments of no thought—just being in the energy. We feel tuned to
the power of lightness, kindness, and connectedness. No separation.
No anger, hate, opinions, evil, or darkness. No fear. And when we
finish our practice and open our eyes, it's time to enter the world with
renewed hope, calmness, and acceptance.

*   *   *

The practice of meditation can open doors to a more loving, peaceful, and fulfilling life. Closing your eyes and sitting in silence for a few
minutes each day can change your life. It changed mine.

Just One Habit to
Deepen Your Meditation Experience

The reward is well worth the effort

Before discussing the one essential habit for a deeper experience in meditation, I want to acknowledge how fortunate anyone is who can sit quietly and meditate in the peace and safety of their home. Many people can't—like the millions in Ukraine right now. My heart aches for them, including a group of young men and women who are my clients and my friends living in Lviv, Ukraine, with their lives shattered, like millions of others. It makes me sick to my stomach that we have to deal with another war. I pray for peace.

With the residue of anger and sadness about Ukraine still in the back of my mind, I sat in the stillness of my living room this morning and meditated, free from worry about being bombed or killed. I got comfortable, closed my eyes, gazed gently ahead, and placed my attention on my breathing. I followed the rise and fall of my lungs—and my mind wandered off. I brought it back, only to find myself lost in random thought again. Back to the breath—making a conscious effort to stay with it. I felt my body on the chair, my right wrist itching. I crossed my legs and then uncrossed them. At least five minutes went by. When the body isn't comfortable, I've found it impossible to go deep into meditation. My awareness gets stuck at the physical level. My mind was flittering away about what to write about—my friends in Ukraine, where the cat was, what I dreamt about last night. I continued breathing slowly from my belly, with intention. Nothing seemed to be happening except the effort of focusing on my breath. I was in Stage One of my typical meditation process—physical awareness.

My awareness gradually shifted from feeling my lungs rising and filling with air to noticing my thoughts. I started to enter Stage

Two—mental awareness. Noticing my thoughts indicates I've started to disconnect from merging with the uncontrollable rascals. However, they persisted and seemed to grow in number and strength. Back to the breath for some help. Then, I started to feel a subtle vibration. The thoughts were fewer and offered less allure. Then, when swept up by one, I returned to the present moment more quickly than before. I continued in this transition state for another five or 10 minutes.

Then I entered the third stage—spiritual awareness. Soft energy swelled before my closed eyes and pushed out the more potent thoughts. I became the observer, witnessing a soft light show, the swirl of the galaxy-like sparks within, the gentle pulse of a seemingly endless force of consciousness. Stillness filled me with the occasional thought peeking in from the back of my mind, sidelined by the soft hand of God-energy. Here's how I describe the light-energy of consciousness dispelling the thinking mind:

> *Visualize a dark room. Now, light a candle, and as the flame begins to burn, watch the light dispel the darkness nearby. Gradually the light fills the space—chasing bits of it hiding in corners. There's nothing aggressive about it—just a gentle, unrelenting power. It eliminates darkness by filling the space with its presence. The nature of consciousness naturally displaces darkness.*

I sat in my happy place absorbing life-giving energy like I was in a bath. There was nothing for me to do except be a recipient. Thoughts? Ego? Virtually not there, but close by for sure—a delicate peace for me. I haven't mastered this fine art. I'm just a student, learning and in awe of what's happening inside me. I gazed into the inner cosmos, letting it fill me up with peace and happiness. Incredible. And it's there, within us all the time. I felt a gentle smile on my face. Why does this feel like home? Because it is my home, and it is your home, too. So, what habit enables me to get through the first two phases of my practice into the third phase?

The habit of patience

Let's face it. Sitting still and doing nothing is not necessarily easy. The human mind is a thought machine. Its job is to think, and when you sit in meditation, you can see this more clearly than ever. The point of meditation is not to stop thinking. The point is to tap into the life-giving energy that keeps us alive, absorb its goodness, and allow it to do its magic. It's like going to a luxurious resort built into the side of a mountain overlooking the Caribbean. Your room is built into a tree; the warm wind lulls you to sleep at night. The sand is pure white; the water is like a warm bath; the fresh food, incredible.

You take it all in. It's restorative; you forget about everything back at home: no texts, no phone calls, no nothing. You're in peace. That's the experience of going deeper into meditation—you let it nurture and heal you.

For me, 15 minutes is generally not enough. It takes 30 minutes or more to go deep. If you want the real thing, you've got to develop patience. Nothing else is going to get through the "mindfield." It takes patience to stop squirming around, uncrossing your legs and crossing them again. It takes patience to continue to sit there when your mind is screaming at you, telling you to get up and get to work. It takes patience to ignore the sounds around you, the smell of coffee wafting into the room, the cat meowing, and the cars passing by on the street. It takes patience to wade through the barrage of doubts your mind is throwing at you. *Nothing is happening. This is a colossal waste of time.* It takes patience to slow the mind down. The mind isn't interested in meditation. The mind wants to think and be in charge.

It takes patience to accomplish anything worthwhile. Playing guitar, painting with watercolors, learning a new language, or mastering online writing—it doesn't matter what it is. It's common to think you should be further along than you are, and it happens in meditation. You think you should be swimming in the ocean of bliss every time you practice. But it's not about what you think or expect. It's about putting in the reps, putting in the time.

Don't give up. If you stick with your practice, you will develop patience, and patience will unlock the deeper experiences in meditation. Patience will serve you in all aspects of life. Waiting on the phone for 20 minutes when you call your bank's customer service department? Practice patience. Standing in a long line at the checkout counter at the grocery store? Practice patience. Dealing with a difficult person at work? Practice patience.

After about 30 minutes, it was time to close my formal practice. I slowly opened my eyes and whispered a prayer of thanks. Then I asked myself a question: "What goal do I pursue today?" The answer: I pursue the path of peace, kindness, and compassion. These are the qualities a consistent meditation practice produces. They're good for me, they're good for you, and we certainly need more of them in the world today.

*   *   *

So, be patient in your practice. The reward is well worth your effort.

The Importance of *Being* in a World Consumed with Doing

Reminders for the spiritual warrior

After a beautiful journey into the great inner stillness, I finished my 30-minute morning meditation practice, opened my eyes, and returned to everyday reality. I wondered why I didn't stay longer in the pure experience of contentment—something that we yearn for so profoundly. I thought about it for several days and concluded that we go within and touch the Divine for two reasons: for our inner fulfillment and to bring the spirit of richness and fulfillment we find there to the world.

When we light ourselves up from the inside, we become beacons of illumination, inspiration, and hope, reminding ourselves and others about the importance of a healthy inner being in a busy world. Without a rich sense of being, finding lasting fulfillment through doing is impossible.

Each day as I go about my business, I do my best to continue my open-eye practice, being mindful and aware of my breath. But honestly, even after 50 years of practicing meditation, it's easy to get consumed with everyday life and lose a solid inner connection. "Living in the moment"—a phrase we often hear these days—isn't always as easy as it might sound. Perhaps it's a walk in the park for the enlightened (whoever they may be), but as an average guy trying to get through the day in one piece, I often find it very challenging.

I read a LinkedIn post by a friend describing her struggle between working flat out, getting stuff done, "doing," and spending time recharging, reflecting, meditating, and "being." I sincerely empathize with her and the challenge she bravely describes. I've edited her post for brevity:

"If I'm being honest, I felt a lot of guilt. I cleared my calendar on Monday and Tuesday to just think. Mission accomplished, but not without big bouts of guilt.

"I intentionally carved out time to do deep work without interruption, and I felt like a bad consultant. Several times I was worried that my clients would find me out and think I wasn't working hard enough.

"I had fights with my inner critic several times a day; she was 'shoulding' all over me—If you're not back to back in meetings, what are you really doing? You're not working as hard as others."

I commented on her post: "We're programmed to believe doing is more important than being. We need to do both with the clear understanding that without a rich connection to our being, we will continue to believe life is all about the doing."

The more we understand our being, the more we make wise choices about how much we need or want to do. The obsession for doing comes from believing we should do it. However, consistent inner practice will reveal that we don't have to struggle as much as we think. It also helps us live more in the ever-elusive present moment, where being conscious and alert enables us to pay attention to life as it happens in real time. The more we live in real time, the more we tap into our intuition, our sixth sense, the more we can make wise decisions about what we do and say.

All of us, whether or not we are warriors, have a cubic centimeter of chance that pops out in front of our eyes from time to time. The difference between an average human and a warrior is that the warrior is aware of this, and one of their tasks is to be alert, deliberately waiting, so that when their cubic centimeter pops out they have the necessary speed, the prowess, to pick it up.

—CARLOS CASTANEDA

Warriors know that the first thing to be conquered is their egoic minds. So they go into the symbolic "cave" not to slay a fire-breathing monster but to calm their inner demons. When I first began to practice raja yoga (royal union) 50 years ago, an ancient, straightforward but effective way to tame the overly talkative and often destructive egoic mind, I found myself in an internal battle. Part of me wanted nothing to do with closing my eyes, following my breath, and sitting in the lotus posture for hours. The other part of me knew this was the most important thing I could ever do.

Which part to listen to? The part that says meditation is a colossal waste of time, a giant escape from reality? Or the part that aches for inner quiet and contentment? I kept leaning into the latter, and I can't tell you how glad I am that I persevered through the unbelievable excuses and distractions created by that part of us that has the most to lose from practicing meditation—the ego. It doesn't want to give up its influence over us.

The warrior's path isn't easy because we must confront our doubts, fears, and weaknesses. They loom in front of us like dark clouds as we attempt to slow down and go within—something not particularly valued or understood by society. But let's remember we're not here to be accountable to society. We're here to enjoy our life and contribute to making the world a better, healthier, and safer place. We can do that by not allowing ourselves to become seduced by the false promises of a world often gone mad. We can do that by regularly giving attention to our *being*.

*   *   *

More doing does not make a better being. More being makes a better being, better doing, and a better life. The doing takes care of itself.

Tips for More Inner Quiet

Practical steps to be more peaceful

Noise. It's all around—barking dogs, ambulance sirens, lawn-mowers, the late-night laughter from a party at your neigh-bor's. But, while often disturbing, it's nothing compared to the noise in our heads: the mental chatter, the commentary, the voices speaking to us, day in and day out. I had a lot of activity in my head, particularly in my early 20s. I couldn't quiet it down; it was as if there were two of me in there constantly talking to each other. The repet-itive thoughts were the worst. When I woke up in the morning, the voice was there, haunting me like a house guest that wouldn't leave. I often thought I was damaged goods. Maybe I was.

Thankfully I learned to meditate, and over the years, the repet-itive voices disappeared. I discovered an essential part of myself through consistent practice, and that inner sanctuary of quiet became a trusted friend—loving, dependable, nonjudgmental, and always there for me. During a recent meditation practice, I slipped into what felt like a quiet underground chamber. No chatter. No noise—just silence and a subtle but all-encompassing energy, vibrating, filling me up with soft, gentle light. I felt like I was swimming in a great pool of consciousness that was bubbling with life and warmth. I remained there for a while, in the absence of thought, in the stillness of the pres-ent moment, and with a glimpse into timelessness.

Eventually, I gently opened my eyes and looked around. I was back in my living room, sitting in my favorite chair, looking at my feet resting on an ottoman. Where had I been? The everyday self, the guy with phone calls to make, articles to write, and broccoli soup to prepare. Did I wander into the Elysian Fields for a brief visit? Or did I disappear into a spiritual experience of "la petite mort"? Perhaps I submerged into a bath of universal consciousness?

I don't know, but I do know my separateness—the "I" within me—was gone for a short time. There was no past or future because thinking became pure feeling. I existed in the present moment, in the experience of nothingness. Totally free—free from the past, free from the future, free of any concern about anything.

How can an experience like that not be healing for our over-worked, over-amped, and overloaded psyche? Unfortunately, most of the messages we absorb every day don't contribute to a healthy psyche or encourage the pursuit of inner peace. Instead, many messages lead us to believe peace is either not important or impossible. But in my experience, both points are false. Inner peace is the most important thing in life, and it is possible to experience it.

So, how do we maintain perspective in a world that tells us the essential things in life are what we achieve, how much we earn, who we know, what our title is, and how much stuff we have? How do we find peace of mind in a noisy world? We know lasting peace is not in people, places, and things. It's within us, and it's as real as the light of day. It's as close as your next breath. The true self, the keeper of inner peace, exists within us all the time, but when we don't turn to it, it lies dormant, remaining just a novel idea or something we'll get around to in the future.

We don't find it by looking outside ourselves but by literally look-ing in the opposite direction. Within us, in the darkness, there is light. Within us, in the nothingness, there is everything. Within us, in the silence, is the sound of our own being, where you'll find the real you: the you that is free from beliefs, free from programming, free from pressure, free from your expectations and those of others.

Tips for more inner quiet

Unplug. The inward journey is more successful when you unplug from what is wearing you out, bringing you down, or winding you up. Unplugging means identifying situations, people, and behavior patterns within your control and making conscious choices about what is good for you. For example, when you're at a restaurant with your partner, if they get up to use the restroom, don't immediately pick up your phone. Give yourself a break. Observe what's going on in the restaurant. It can be a hard habit to break, but it's an excellent way to practice unplugging. If you can't resist the urge to pick up your phone, you've got an addiction, something for you to work on.

Try keeping your cellphone and other devices out of your bedroom a few nights a week and see what happens to your sleep patterns. Instead of reading every book on your Kindle or iPad, try reading a soft or hardcover book. There's something very relaxing about it. Draw firm boundaries with people that drain your energy. Limit your time with them; cut your ties if necessary.

Sit in silence. The purpose of doing this is to get used to slowing down and doing nothing. Start with five minutes once a day and increase if it feels right. Sit comfortably and focus on your breath, inhaling and exhaling slowly and deeply through your nose. When your mind wanders, gently bring it back to your breath.

Notice your inner talk. Begin by observing your thoughts; they're like passing clouds—they come, and they go. They aren't the real you. The real you is the watcher of your thoughts, and that is where you will find inner peace. The more you observe, the more separation from the talkative, ego-centric mind you create; the more separation you create, the easier it will be to go deeper when you practice meditation.

Reframe automatic negative thoughts (ANTs). We all have thought patterns. They often show up like uninvited guests at a cocktail party—you didn't ask for them, but they appear, and some of them are negative and manifest as limiting beliefs. If you notice a thought like *"I'm not good enough,"* then replace it with *"I'm perfect the way I am."* Repeat that to yourself. Say it out loud if you can. If you hear *"I can't do that,"* replace it with *"I can do anything I put my mind to."*

Use sources of inspiration. Listen to, read, or watch something that uplifts you on a regular basis. Absorbing five or ten minutes of positive messaging per day can rewire your brain. For example, I listened to 21 short podcasts by Deepak Chopra about abundance, and they shifted my entire mindset. A week into the sessions, I felt a change in my brain that has not regressed since. Positive messages can be antidotes to any negativity you might pick up throughout the day.

Create a regular meditation practice. There are many ways to do this. You can do it all on your own by reading books, downloading one of the many apps available, or finding videos on YouTube, or you can look for a guru or teacher to help you. I found a teacher many years ago whose guidance has been invaluable. My writer friend, David Gerken, has a great free guide on his website about building a meditation practice.

Carve out white space. We live in a switched-on, achievement-oriented world, with many of us working longer and harder than ever. It's not a good recipe for long-term health or happiness. On the other hand, when we slow down and do less, we open up space for our brains to rest, be healthier, and be more creative. White space gives us more time to *be;* it allows us to be more present and attentive. It also helps us accept things we can't change and makes it easier to live more harmoniously with ourselves and others.

Create white space by getting out in nature more often, sitting in silence, meditating, journaling, saying No to things that cannibalize your free time, being clear on your priorities, identifying your core values and living by them and engaging in creative hobbies like painting, music, or dance.

*   *   *

There is peace behind all the noise. You deserve to find it.

PART 6

Navigating
the Business World

How to Get Deeper Meaning
in Work and Life

Ask yourself one essential question to unlock the answer

f I asked what you do for a living, you'd tell me what your job is,
right? For example, you might be a software engineer, barista,
writer, real estate agent, or customer service rep. But your role or
title is not your real job. Your real job is something else—something
much more significant.

Now, I'm not going to change your mind about what you do for
a living. But, by the time you finish this essay, *you* will think about it
differently and you will realize that your change in perspective can
transform your outlook on life, including your personal and professional relationships.

It might sound a bit over the top, but I'm not kidding. Stay with me.

First, as you know, we live in an achievement-oriented world
where the emphasis is on what we do, the role we play, or the title
on our business cards. Societal success is measured mainly by how
much we earn, where we live, what kind of car we drive, who our
friends are, and so on.

We identify with our role and profession and work hard to get
good at it. And so we should. But when we *only* identify with what we
do, we severely limit our personal and professional potential.

What is your job?

Our job is not what we do—*it's the goal we pursue.*

What's the job of a teacher? To teach, right? *No.*

A teacher's job is to *help their students learn.*

What is a sales manager's job? To manage all those pesky
salespeople, right? *No.*

A sales manager's job is to help each team member grow and succeed.

What's the job of the guy who cleans your gym? To keep the gym clean, right? *No.*

His job is to help create an environment where people feel safe and looked after.

A teacher's focus

It's more expansive when a teacher defines their job as helping students learn. The focus is on their students, not on themselves. If a teacher believes their job is to teach, the focus is on them. It's a narrow point of view that plays right into the belief that the world revolves around them. They are the mighty teacher, the authority figure, the keeper, and the dispenser of wisdom.

I've known too many teachers more concerned about plowing through the lesson plan than how well anyone was learning. But success at anything can't be measured simply by what you do; it must be measured by the impact you make.

Of all the teachers I've had through grade school, high school, and university, one stands out. My high school English teacher, Joel Kabatznick, whom I wrote about in the first article in this book, knew his job was to help his students learn. His self-deprecating humor, quirky clothes, humble attitude, and zest for life created a safe environment where learning was fun. As a result, students loved and trusted him and consequently were more receptive to learning.

Joel made an indelible impact on me; after all, here I am, writing about him 60 years later. His great work in the classroom flowed like water from his heart. He had a crystal-clear understanding of his job.

Joel understood one of life's big secrets—if you get your "being" right, your "doing" will take of itself. He didn't have to be an authority figure, helping a bunch of kids with raging hormones find a way to appreciate English literature. He simply knew he was there to be of service to his students' education. And we did learn. Many of us never forgot the example of a man who was clear about the goal he pursued—to help his students learn.

Here's how being clear about your goal can help you make a positive difference in the world.

Two examples of clarifying the pursuit of your goal

Suppose I'm a barista. Conventional thinking says my job is to make lattes and cappuccinos. True. But what goal can I pursue that involves making great cups of coffee but is more expansive?

How about this: My job is to create a delightful, memorable experience for my customers. And if that is the goal I pursue, then I will make great lattes *and* do my best to connect with customers on a human level with a smile, eye contact, and a pleasant attitude, ensuring they are delighted.

Isn't it a much more expansive point of view than thinking I'm just a barista? And I'll likely stand head and shoulders above anyone who believes their job is just to make lattes. If a manager is looking for people with potential, who will get noticed?

I'm married, and my goal as a partner in the relationship is to be loving, kind, truthful, and supportive. When there is potential for friction, I do my best to ask myself what goal I want to go after. Do I want to fight to be right? Or do I want to follow the path of kindness, humility, open discussion, respect for differences, and help my wife have a great life? If I choose the latter, the attitude helps keep my behavior aligned with my overall intention for how I want to be.

There are times I fail—times when I succumb to my ego. But when I remember to ask myself what goal I pursue, it works every time. And there is peace in the land of Johnsons.

The goals you pursue in your work

When we realize our job is not what's printed on our business card, doors we didn't know existed open for us. Instead of pursuing success as defined by the completion of agreed-upon duties, we seek something more significant—the satisfaction of striving toward our goal *while* carrying out our responsibilities.

You're more likely to be personally satisfied when you pursue a noble goal of service to others because you tap into a unique type of happiness that results from living in alignment with your highest values. No one can take this happiness away from you. It's not dependent on external circumstances you have no control over.

If you work with a team or company, your focus is not winning at any cost, self-promotion, or supporting a functional/silo mentality. You focus on helping the team win. You look for ways to improve things and help others succeed.

By putting the goal you pursue first in your life, you can have greater personal fulfillment, more meaningful connections with others, and enhanced professional achievement. You'll stand out from the crowd, make a positive difference in the world, feel proud of your behavior, and set an example for others.

So, what goal do you pursue?

* * *

The goal you pursue becomes your North Star. It keeps you on the right track. Make that goal first in your life.

How to Recover from Losing Your Identity If You Lose Your Job

Ten Lessons for Coming Back Stronger Than Ever

Losing your job is tough. I lost my job three times when I was working in corporate America. Fired twice; laid off once. I went through phases of fear, anger, resentment, anxiety, depression, hopelessness, physical illness, financial hardship, shame, and guilt for many months at a time. The climb back into full balance and acceptance sometimes took more than a year.

I had to claw my way through each situation. It was hard work, and it didn't seem to matter that I practiced meditation regularly or that I had done mental strength training as part of my tennis career. My knowledge of change management theory or the archetypal pattern of learning described in Joseph Campbell's *Hero's Journey* didn't make me immune to psychological, emotional, physical, and financial difficulties, either.

Suddenly, whatever my business card said no longer applied. *"If I'm not the VP of Sales anymore, who the hell am I?"* I wondered. That was a mind-bender. Within a matter of hours, instead of getting hundreds of emails a day, I was getting none. My status didn't exist anymore. I was no longer "important." Most colleagues simply went about their business as if I had never been there. Very few reached out to see how I was doing. I thought, *"Is this what it's like when you die?"*

Was I a slow learner? Did I enjoy wallowing in my suffering? Or was I terrible at adapting to change? None of the above. My reactions to losing my job were completely normal. Here's what I learned about how to bounce back.

My amygdala (reptilian brain) went into overdrive, defensive mode, telling me my life was at risk. It was doing precisely what it was supposed to do: protect me from threats. Losing your job is undoubtedly a significant threat.

In his brilliant essay, "SCARF: a brain-based model for collaborating with and influencing others," David Rock, co-founder of The NeuroLeadership Institute, wrote: "The perception of a potential or real reduction in status can generate a strong threat response. Eisenberger and colleagues showed that a reduction in status resulting from being left out of an activity lit up the same regions of the brain as physical pain (Eisenberger et al., 2003). While this study explores social rejection, it is closely connected to the experience of a drop in status."

Rock explains that there are five aspects of human social experience: status, certainty, autonomy, relatedness, and fairness. The underlying driver of our behavior, he says, is the deeply embedded desire to reduce threat and increase reward or positive experiences. Let's review these five in the context of job loss:

1. *Status*—With the loss of a job, there's a loss of identity, loss of value in the eyes of others, and shame associated with not having a job, being unemployed, or being furloughed.

2. *Certainty*—With the loss of a job, one has no idea what the future holds and has to deal with questions like: "Will I get unemployment?" "How long will it last?" "Will I get my job back?" "How long will I be furloughed?"

3. *Autonomy*—With the loss of a job, one experiences a loss of control over the current situation. One might not be able to support oneself or one's family financially and might not be able to maintain regular daily routines such as going shopping, visiting with friends, attending sports, playing sports, and going out to eat.

4. *Relatedness*—With the loss of a job, one is no longer a part of the organization and is eliminated from a social network, the work tribe. One finds oneself on the outside looking in. Work relationships fractured.

5. *Fairness*—With the loss of a job, one might feel singled out while the organization still employs other people.

Any or all of these factors trigger a threat response from the brain—and we deal with all five when we lose a job. It's no wonder that losing a job can put us in a tailspin.

Psychiatrist Elizabeth Kübler Ross wrote about the five stages of grief: denial, anger, bargaining, depression, and acceptance in her book, *On Death and Dying*. Author William Bridges outlined three stages of transition—endings, neutral zone, and new beginnings—in *Managing Transitions*. There certainly are differences between the two theories; however, they both point out that we go through predictable patterns when dealing with significant and traumatic change. For anyone going through loss and grief, it's beneficial to understand the process they will likely go through.

I've learned that no matter what those stages are, we need to make good choices to reach the acceptance stage, the new beginning, where we have learned, matured, grown, and found our balance again. If we don't make good choices, we linger in the process and potentially get stuck in resentment or bitterness.

Ten ideas to help you recover and thrive

1. Remember that you're not the title on your business card

As I went through two of my three transitions, I struggled mightily with this idea. I discovered I was deeply attached to my work identity. I managed teams who looked to me for guidance and support, I had long-term positive relationships across the organization, and I was proud of what my colleagues and I had accomplished.

Being a leader of a team wasn't just a job for me. It was something I loved and enjoyed. I was mentally, emotionally, and psychologically invested—always on, working many nights, weekends, and on the road a lot. In fact, I had allowed my job to become who I was rather than what I did professionally. Workaholic? Yes.

Gradually, I felt my attachment to my role dissolve. Honestly, it was one of the most challenging parts of the process. I knew from my meditation practice that I had to peel off the layers of identity and get down to the essence: I am not my title. I am a human being, and I need to get back in touch with who I am.

The process was painful, and it took months to disconnect from my corporate identity. There were reoccurring dreams with the key players responsible for my dismissal. There were replayed conversations in my head and endless "what ifs." I felt like I was shedding my skin—my mask—and rediscovering who I was. Ultimately that served me well. Getting there was just not fun.

What did I do? I shifted my focus from *doing* to *being*. I slowed down, stopped being a workaholic, spent time in reflection, and reconnected to the real me.

2. Focus on what you can control

We always have a choice when it comes to how we behave. During each of my transitions, I knew I was facing a challenge, and I knew the way I responded would determine my future. I could feel sorry for myself or I could pick up the pieces and move on, which is what I did.

During one of my transitions, I started to journal in the mornings, meditated regularly, read inspiring books, and started a blog. I wrote ten articles in six months.

I set small, achievable goals. I felt my confidence grow when I accomplished something. For a job search, I made a list of all the people that I knew and reached out to each one; I set a minimum of five per week. I had many conversations and built some long-lasting relationships.

If I went to an interview, I prepared well. That was in my control. I focused on doing my best, no matter the outcome. There was a time when I felt a bit desperate. I recall a few interviews where the desperation must have been wafting off me like cheap cologne. I didn't get called back. I was disappointed, and all I could do was try to learn from the experience and move on.

What did I do? I worked on my attitude, created a plan, and took action.

3. Let go of resentment

Resentment is defined as bitter indignation at having been treated unfairly. I certainly had a bad case of it once. It's a nasty state of mind when you want to do things you'll only regret later, like write an email to the people that sent you packing and tell them off. Go ahead, write the email, just don't send it. I know people that have done this, and they say it was cathartic and helped them move through resentment into forgiveness and acceptance.

At first, I recall demonizing the people that let me go. My mind made it very personal. *They did something to me and should be punished!* This attitude is the classic victim, "the world is out to get me!" mindset. Remember that it's a phase, a place you are visiting. You don't want to take out a long-term lease on it.

What did I do? I stopped being a victim and played the cards I was dealt to the best of my ability.

4. Focus on learning and growth

Then I shifted my mindset from *"This really sucks"* to *"I have an opportunity to learn and do something new."* I knew that my dark night of the soul would lead to a new and better chapter in my life if I continued to make smart choices regarding how I behaved. I visualized the past as a room with the door closed and saw another door open to a brighter future. I stood in the hallway between these two doors with a choice: I could see my situation as a disaster or as an opportunity to grow and learn. I chose growth and learning.

Then I defined my reason for being, my Ikigai, a Japanese word meaning "reason for being." Ikigai has four components: that which I love, that which I am good at, that which I can be paid for, and that which the world needs.

Then I wrote down my version of those four components and drew them out on paper. Then each morning, I imagined myself doing and having exactly what I wanted. I was practicing active visualization, a powerful method of creating desired outcomes. It has really helped me through each transition.

What did I do? I defined and visualized what I wanted in the future.

5. Be patient

While conventional wisdom says patience is a virtue, I often found it very difficult to practice. I wanted things to operate on my time-table—but life doesn't work that way. With no clear end in sight, I simply had to work on my mindset and stay as optimistic and positive as I could. Anything else was out of my hands.

In 2009, I knew I had serious work to do, given the economic climate and my age. Getting rejected at one interview after the next didn't help. I was hanging in there. The negative self-talk poured in: *"You're 55 years old. No one wants to hire you. You're done, pal."* I just kept at it, accepting that it might take more time than I'd like to find employment again.

I've been through long job searches before but doing so during a recession proved to be a very tough challenge.

Eventually, in 2011, I reconnected with a former colleague who was a general manager at a consulting company and took a job that I was overqualified for. Within a year, I was promoted back into a leadership role. I was on my way again—and deeply grateful.

What did I do? I made a consistent effort and focused on the process, not the outcome.

6. Know and manage your weaknesses

Self-anesthetization became my best friend at times. The mindless distractions took over: binging on the computer, TV, drinking, and unhealthy eating. At one point, I needed an extra recycling bin just to handle all of my empty wine bottles.

I had my bouts with boredom too. In his book, *The Uncharted Journey*, couples therapist Don Rosenthal masterfully describes boredom as an experience of being uncomfortable with one's present reality and seeking distraction to avoid that discomfort.

He writes, "When I allow myself to be bored, I see it as a 'No' to what is. This moment is felt to be without value, except insofar as it can get me quickly to the next moment where the mind believes my satisfaction lies."

Staying very present and living consciously in the moment is undoubtedly tricky when you don't like your circumstances and are not fully engaged in meaningful work. I knew I needed to stay active if I wanted to manage my boredom and not self-medicate. I created projects around the house, started a local networking group—which can be done virtually now—and spent time studying and reading.

I have to tell you, there were times when I didn't manage boredom very well. My impulses sometimes got the better of me, but when they did, I learned to be kinder to myself and forgiving. If I caught myself binging, I wouldn't berate myself; I would say, *"Okay. Time to move on."* I watched my language and eliminated "I should" from my vocabulary. Instead of focusing on what wasn't working, I put my attention on what was working well and celebrated any small achievements.

What did I do? I stayed active, leaned into my strengths, and accepted that it's okay to be bored at times. I stopped telling myself I "should" be making more progress.

7. Don't buy into fear

Fear is like a virus; it needs to feed on something living. Without a host, it can't exist. I could feel fear hovering about, looking for a way into me. Even the smallest fears were carriers of dark energy, like miniature Trojan horses, who disguised themselves as harmless thoughts. If I paid attention to one of them, I was simply welcoming it into my inner world, where it created doom and gloom.

I knew that fear wouldn't exist in me if I didn't listen to it. I found I needed to be hyper-vigilant to any negative self-talk. If I heard any, I'd turn away from it, or I would reframe it. Example: *"Everything is getting worse."* Reframe: *"I am facing a big challenge, and I can do it."* Fear, like darkness, cannot exist in the light. I kept the lights on as much as I could.

What did I do? I practiced meditation, reframed negative self-talk, used positive affirmations, and prayed regularly.

8. Ask for help

I hired a life coach after I got fired the first time. I was quite a miserable person at that period in my life, and the coach did everything he could for someone who was utterly lost and confused. I tried to put into practice the coaching and daily routines he suggested. They did help; it just took time.

In place of a coach, friends that support and challenge you are also invaluable. There's nothing like the care and love that can come from someone who can see what you can't and call you out on what needs to be said. Without a meaningful connection to those you value and trust, it's too easy to contract and withdraw when things aren't going well. I learned I had to make an effort to reach out, despite how difficult that was.

What did I do? I reached out to friends and colleagues.

9. Balance realism with optimism

The principle of balancing realism with optimism, known as The Stockdale Paradox, was made famous by Jim Collings in his masterpiece *Good to Great,* in which he described the philosophy of former vice-presidential candidate and a Vietnam prisoner of war, Jim Stockdale, who was tortured repeatedly over seven years.

Stockdale said, "You must never confuse faith that you will prevail in the end—which you can never afford to lose—with the discipline to confront the most brutal facts of your current reality, whatever they might be." I had to confront my brutal facts: I did not have a job, my savings were diminishing, and I was struggling through the transition process. But I also had a strong track record and reputation in the industry and many useful contacts.

My faith helped me believe I would get through it and everything would be okay. Understanding both principles helped me maintain my sanity and positive outlook.

What did I do? I never gave up.

10. Build Resilience

Cy Wakeman, *New York Times* best-selling author, tells this story:

> "We did this great experiment that I used when I was teaching a college course. We put third- and fourth-grade children in a gym, turned the lights off, and watched how they behaved. Then we put only adults in a gym; we turned the lights off and watched how they behaved. The difference we saw was amazing.

> "When the lights went out on the adults, they sat quietly, isolated, without reaching out for one another. They waited for one or two innovative people to come along and figure out what might have gone wrong. They were so well behaved that they hardly moved from their spot.

> "When the third and fourth graders experienced the lights going off, they moved from their spot and reached out to others. It was hilarious! They were trying to figure out who was beside them by feeling each other's hair and asking their teachers who might have a cellphone.

> "They were thinking about reaching out and connecting with others. They were very noisy and very extroverted. They were grabbing ahold of others, sticking together, looking beyond themselves. You see that while the adults sat alone, quietly persevering, the children were resilient."

Perseverance is "the continued effort to do or achieve something despite difficulties, failure, or opposition." Resilience is "an ability to recover from or adjust easily to misfortune or change." Isn't there something loving and intelligent about small children reaching out in the dark to each other? Are we not in the "dark" when we lose our job? Yes, we are, and perhaps if we behave like the children in Wakeman's story—reaching out and connecting with others—we'll land on our feet more quickly.

What did I do? I accepted my circumstances, practiced gratitude for what I did have, and reached out to former friends and colleagues on a regular basis.

* * *

And let's remember what Nelson Mandela said: "It's always impossible until it's done."

Five Simple,
Powerful Leadership Principles

Common sense goes a long way

What you do and say creates your reputation and character, whether you are a CEO, parent, writer, or plumber. Your aspirations, dreams, intentions, vision circles, task lists, and values don't matter. We all have good intentions, and sometimes we get off track and do or say things we wish we hadn't.

Many things contribute to success in life and business, yet perhaps what's most important is the ability to stay on track.

Jack Zenger and Dale Miller, founders of global leadership development firm Zenger-Miller, who worked with more than half of the Fortune 500 at the time, developed a set of five principles they called The Basic Principles. They have been used in executive boardrooms, factory floors, and call centers for over thirty years and have helped hundreds of thousands of people around the world stay on track. They have been helping people and companies be more successful, and they are as relevant today as ever.

Zenger-Miller's Basic Principles

1. Focus on the issue, situation, or behavior, not the person

Be objective and factual. "You agreed to return my call by Friday, and I didn't hear from you until Tuesday. What happened?" Facts are friendly but avoid making assumptions based on circumstantial evidence. Don't pre-judge the situation without getting all relevant points of view. Drawing conclusions regarding someone's intent is risky business. We can't see intention, but we can see what someone does. Remain neutral and calm when problem-solving. "I'm not sure what you had in mind, but what I heard you say to your colleague sounded very aggressive. What happened?"

Not focusing on the person means leaving anything like a person's attitude, beliefs, or personality out of the conversation. "I don't like your attitude" or "That's a stupid idea" are useless comments and argument starters. If you don't like someone's attitude, ask yourself, what did they do or say that makes me think this way? Discuss what you observed or heard. Focus on the facts, not on personality.

2. Help support others' self-confidence and self-esteem

We all want to be seen, heard, acknowledged, and treated fairly. Accurate, fact-based dialogue supports a fair and respectful atmosphere. If we unfairly criticize, demean, or threaten, we undermine others. Being too harsh or brutally honest serves no collaborative purpose other than tearing someone down. For example, describing someone that comes in late for work as "checked out" is demeaning, judgmental, and a surefire way to attack their self-esteem. A more effective approach is to stick to fact-based dialogue and genuine curiosity by saying, "I've noticed you've been late by 20 minutes three times this week. What's going on?"

Sarcasm, backhanded compliments, and statements like "I was just kidding" are toxic and destructive, too.

We are emotional and intuitive beings. We might not remember everything someone said, but we do remember how they made us feel. When we listen, acknowledge, and speak with truthfulness and kindness, people around us will thrive, and they will remember how we treated them.

3. Build and maintain constructive relationships

A team or organization's success depends on the degree of trust, conflict management, commitment, and accountability. Providing recognition, respecting differences, giving developmental feedback, offering a stretch project, or asking for input are just a few simple ways to build more connections and strengthen group relationships.

Much of the same applies to personal and family relationships as well. The way we speak to our partner or children creates the type of relationship we will have. You decide: Acrimonious, sarcastic, or nit-picky? Or caring, considerate, and thoughtful? Which will lead to the relationship you want? It's the little things that make a big difference.

Withholding information, lying by exception, and spreading gossip and rumors will destroy a relationship or team. Being authentic, honest, transparent, and thoughtful will instead build healthy relationships.

When our desired outcome for any interaction is to build and maintain the relationship, we will behave accordingly. If we don't care about the relationship, we will approach it quite differently, and the results will speak for themselves.

4. Take the initiative to make things better

Our attitude has more impact on our lives than our intelligence. We choose our response in any given situation. A positive mental attitude and/or a growth mindset makes situations decidedly better as opposed to complaining or waiting for others to act. A growth mindset sees challenges as opportunities and persists in the face of setbacks. It prioritizes learning over seeking approval and learns to give and receive constructive feedback. Above all, a growth mindset acknowledges and embraces its weaknesses.

A mixed mindset blames others, avoids responsibility, and gives up quickly. It shies away from the unknown and sees itself as powerless. It can't take the initiative. But, when you commit to growth and learning, you naturally take the initiative to make things better and encourage others to do the same.

5. Lead by example

There's nothing worse than people saying one thing and doing something else. It's the fastest way to destroy anyone's reputation and credibility. And there's nothing more powerful than setting an example for others. By watching others, we learn what is acceptable, how to fit in, and what is important. Everyday lead-by-examples include:

> Keeping and honoring your commitments
>
> Telling the truth, even if it is painful
>
> Admitting when you are wrong
>
> Listening without interruption
>
> Being kind to yourself and others
>
> Leaving things better than you found them
>
> Showing up on time
>
> Saying thank you when receiving a compliment.

*   *   *

Focus on the issue, situation, or behavior, not the person. Maintain the self-confidence and self-esteem of others. Build and maintain constructive relationships. Take the initiative to make things better. Lead by example. Yes, these are common-sense practices. Make them common practice, and you can't go wrong.

How to Quickly Size Up
Someone's Personality Style

Simple tools that can help

A few years ago, a colleague sat in our newly formed leadership team meeting, his forehead all scrunched up. I imagined the three-bean chili he had for lunch was rebelling, or maybe he just had chronic angst. As the head of marketing finished her update, the team launched into a lively discussion—everyone but scrunch face.

He remained that way for the rest of the meeting, not saying a word. My inside voice churned: *"He'd be great at a museum, guarding ancient paintings. I thought the chili was rather tasty. Maybe he doesn't like the head of marketing. Will he ever speak?"* When the meeting ended, I asked someone who knew him well what was up. "Oh," she said. "When he looks like that, he's just thinking." *"Really? Thinking?"* I wondered. *"Can't he think and speak at the same time?"*

A few weeks later, I met him. We discussed our communication preferences and how to best work together. I learned he was introverted—*really* introverted. He needed time to think and process and didn't like speaking up in meetings unless he was well prepared. And—he loved details, which were not my strong suit. I shared my style with him—talkative, outgoing, sociable, persuasive, and action-oriented. We were almost exact opposites.

I saw my judgments and biases for what they were—made up stories and misconceptions, mainly because his demeanor and communication style were so different from mine. As time went on, I learned how to work with him. Before meetings, I emailed him questions so that he'd have time to think. He spoke up more in meetings and seemed more relaxed. He brought humor into our discussions and his presentations. He adjusted his approach, and so did I. Over the following months, our skills meshed well, and we became good colleagues and friends.

Working well together isn't always easy but understanding a few core things about people's personalities and communication styles is. And they can make a big difference when it comes to building strong relationships. Here's a process, based on Jungian psychological theory, that helps:

Answer These Questions

1. Does this person think to speak (quiet, introverted) or do they speak to think (talkative, extroverted)?

2. Are they more formal and task-focused (thinking) or are they more informal and relationship-focused (feeling)?

The first question helps determine if someone tends toward introversion or extroversion. Introverts prefer to gain or recharge their energy by going inwards. Extroverts tend to be more active and engage with the world around them. The question gets at their decision-making style. Is it more formal, impersonal, and objective or more informal, personal, and subjective? Do they think more than feel (Are they more head than heart?) or vice-versa?

Try this. Draw a line down the middle of a piece of paper. The left-hand side will refer to introversion, and the right-hand side will refer to extroversion. Then draw a horizontal line, putting "thinking" above it and "feeling" below it.

The graph depicts four basic styles or preferences. Everyone has all of them, but typically one is dominant. The key to understanding someone's communication style is knowing their dominant preference. That is the purpose of the questions.

For example, someone that's an extroverted thinker typically prefers a factual, fast, and straightforward approach to receiving

Introverted and Thinking	Extroverted and Thinking
Introverted and Feeling	Extroverted and Feeling

information. If you give them a long-winded, meandering stream of information, they will likely get bored and irritated. They want the headline and then supporting information laid out logically and quickly. Conversely, someone who tends to be more quiet, thoughtful, and sensitive may not appreciate a straightforward, impersonal manner with demands for a quick decision. They want a more personal, caring approach, and they might need time to reflect and think before making a decision. Breakdowns in connection occur when our preferences are ignored or not recognized.

We can detect someone's style by observing speech patterns, body language, office decor, and personal appearance. We can also pick up clues through email or texts. For example, long, wordy emails or texts with many emoticons can be clues of a feeling preference. Short, crisp, and impersonal messages can indicate more of a thinking preference.

Characteristics of each style

- *Extroverted thinking* people are bold, assertive, results-driven, action-oriented, and determined.

- *Extroverted feeling* people are sociable, dynamic, demonstrative, enthusiastic, and persuasive.

¤ *Introverted feeling* people are collaborative, encouraging, mentoring, patient, and relaxed.

¤ *Introverted thinking* people are analytical, precise, cautious, detail-oriented, and formal.

How to communicate with each style

Once you've determined someone's dominant interactive style, follow these suggestions for communicating with them:

¤ *Extroverted Thinking:* Be direct and to the point. Focus on results. Be confident and assertive. Don't hesitate, be indecisive, focus on feelings, or try to take over.

¤ *Introverted Feeling:* Be patient and supportive. Ask for input before you make a decision. Ask for their opinion and give them time to answer. Don't take advantage of their good nature. Don't push them to make quick decisions; don't tell, instruct, or command.

¤ *Extroverted Feeling:* Be friendly, sociable, engaging, and stimulating. Be open and flexible. Don't bore them with details, tie them down with routine, or ask them to work alone for long periods.

¤ *Introverted Thinking:* Be well prepared and thorough. Put things in writing and let them consider all the details. Don't be over-emotional or exaggerate, and don't careless or casual with important issues.

Practical next steps

Start with yourself: What preference are you?

Action: Make a list of the people you interact with most frequently—your coworkers, your boss, your partner, or your spouse. What clues can help you identify their style?

Action: Have a conversation with someone you trust about your style, their style, and the best way to communicate with them. Or try an approach that seems to match their style and ask for feedback.

*   *   *

We all want to be seen, heard, and appreciated. Adjusting your style when you're interacting with others sends a powerful message that you care for and respect them. They'll be more likely to be loyal, creative, and productive in return. Who wouldn't want that?

How to Survive the
Dark Side of Corporate Life

Here's how not to get caught with your pants down

In 2009, I was working on a coaching project with some of Sheryl Sandberg's Ad Sense managers at Google's Mountain View campus. At one of our meetings, I looked around the room and realized I was the oldest guy there. I was 58. *"How the hell did this happen?"* I thought. *"Do all these young, intelligent millionaires notice, too? Oh. Yeah, they do."* Every slumbering insecurity about my age woke up at the same time. I started dyeing my hair blond on the advice of my hairdresser. He said, "Don't go darker—go lighter. Darker on a man looks more desperate, not to mention ridiculous." Right. Turn me into a blond now, please.

It was clear—I'd crossed life's midpoint and was now a target for ads selling reverse mortgages, cremation packages, and cereal with extra fiber. Yes, I was a bit desperate; getting old wasn't something I was ready to fully accept at the time. So, I kept it at a distance for the next ten years and did my best to look younger. Maybe it was because I was fighting off the inevitable, or maybe I was just uptight and insecure. Or maybe it was because I was in corporate America and afraid of being ushered out the door in favor of younger human resources.

Seven lessons learned from more than 30 years of working in corporate America

1. We are human resources.

Many wonderful organizations in the world today are doing amazing things and are run by people trying to do their best. But when leadership is weak and gives nothing but lip service to their espoused corporate values while behaving like mercenaries, the people who are their human "resources" (terrible label, by the way) get treated more like objects and less like human beings. Things go out of whack fast at that point. When profits take precedence over people—something no one will admit to at the time—people get treated just like any other resource.

When someone decides this particular resource is no longer useful, it's given a certain spin: "Tom has left the organization to pursue other opportunities." I'll tell you what Tom is doing—he's signing up for unemployment and scrambling like crazy to find another job. Not to mention going to a shrink to get over the trauma of his whole life suddenly being turned upside down.

People forget that one of the jobs of the department of human resources is to protect the company from legal trouble. Companies don't like to get sued or lose discrimination lawsuits, so they quietly settle for sizable amounts of money to stay out of court. One big lost lawsuit can sink a small company. Human resources can be your friend as long as you are in the favor of those in power. However, when you fall out of favor, your friends in human resources quickly become the people trying to get you out the door, paying you the minimum severance they can get away with. They're not your friends anymore—they have a job to do, and it is to protect the company's assets. You are the problem that needs to quietly fade away as quickly as possible.

2. Unconscious biases are everywhere.

I've held senior leadership roles in three well-known performance-improvement companies. Each company did its best to create environments that respected diversity of all kinds. Still, it's almost impossible to shut down the unconscious biases running behind the scenes. Some people were worse than others. They did and said things they shouldn't have. I sat in meetings and listened to utter garbage come out of people's mouths who held the lives and careers of others in their hands. "Oh, she's getting old, isn't she? I bet she's slowing down. Might be time for her to go." I heard those words about one of my salespeople who was the same age as me. Funny, the person that said it is now long gone—fired like a torpedo off a submarine. And the salesperson? Still there. Humming away like there's no tomorrow. Energy? Got more than ever. Botox? Plenty of that, too, and it's working just fine.

I hope she rocks on until she's 75 or more.

3. Don't get caught up in image obsession.

I found corporate America to be obsessed with image. Sadly, many managers hire in their own image. They look for people who look, think, and act as they do. They realize it eventually, but not until they've filled up the team with clones of themselves. It's not always the best strategy.

I fell victim to the practice for my first few years as a new manager, unaware I was doing this. Eventually, I saw the problem and then used a hiring process that helped eliminate or at least reduce any biases. After that, things seemed to go better until a new, younger leader came in who was very concerned with image. He cleaned the house of anyone who didn't "look" the part. Tragic. A lot of really good people hit the streets.

So, yes, this is why we try to look younger as we get older. We know we have to play the game because we're swimming in a shark tank and need all the anti-shark protection we can get.

4. You are replaceable at any time.

When I left my last full-time job, I was "retired" by those who wanted me gone. I got one of those "Thank you for everything you have done for the company" email announcements that everyone knows is a polite way of saying don't let the door hit you on the way out. I'd served my purpose. The previous five years had been delightful and successful—I enjoyed my colleagues on the leadership team, and revenue grew exponentially. However, the last nine months were a disaster. I was cleverly used during a period of organizational transition, and when certain objectives were achieved, I was unceremoniously given the proverbial boot right out the door.

It took another nine months for me to unload all the stress, anxiety, and trauma of the incident. Overly identified with my job, I had to detangle myself. I know plenty of others who had the same experience as I did. I felt like a disposable lighter. I had served my purpose, and then I was tossed away in favor of a newer, younger, and less expensive model.

I also want to say that I'm grateful for all the jobs I've held. But sometimes, it's time to move on. My issue isn't about what's done when people need to leave the business; my issue is how it's done. The lack of humanity and empathy is often astounding.

5. When you swim with sharks, you are likely to become one.

I tried hard not to get sucked into organizational politics and game-playing. However, if you wind up in senior management, you are responsible for making your boss look good, and if the boss is the CEO or an executive team member and wants somebody fired, you either do it or resign. I joined a well-known firm as a sales leader midway through my career, and when I met with my new boss, the senior VP of sales, for the first time, we exchanged a few niceties, and then he closed the door. He told me the first thing he wanted me to do was fire a certain salesperson. A few weeks later, I showed her the way out with as much care as possible. I behaved like a shark.

6. Beware the shadow of the organization.

Most of us have parts of ourselves we keep on a short leash—our wounds and childhood traumas that inform our attitudes, values, beliefs, and biases. These wounds are our shadows; they don't heal up by our ignoring them or pretending they don't exist. That just makes them stronger. They follow us around wherever we go until we bring them into the light and deal with them.

Organizations are made up of many people that are a collection of everyone's shadow. The more dysfunctional an organization, the bigger the shadow. Lots of pressure and stress in the organization? Lots of passive-aggressive and other strange behavior shows up.

Here's an example of an organizational shadow I experienced. I was part of a company that put incredible effort into promoting a people-focused culture where you could bring your whole self to work. The problem was, when you scratched below the surface, they treated people poorly, and the churn in and out the door was horrendous. There was a lot of talk and good intentions, but in reality it was all about the money. People first? Nope. Money first; people second. All organizational dysfunction starts at the top, and in this instance, there was plenty of it up there.

7. Functions can cause friction.

Most organizations consist of departments and functions that often operate like mini kingdoms. Sales, finance, engineering, legal. Silos. Separate entities with distinct goals and objectives. On the one hand, it's all well and good, but organizations get paralyzed by internal bickering between functions way too often. I've seen politics and backstabbing in almost every executive team I've been on or worked with, and it was because people were protecting their all-important functional kingdom.

Functions play right into the hands of people who would do anything to make their team look good—often at the expense of other functions and teams. Sales and marketing clash. Legal and operations disagree. The amount of time wasted because of internal B.S. is staggering. Most key performance indicators incent individual and functional success. Unfortunately, it's a rare organization that has cracked the code on integrating company-wide and functional incentives. The friction at the top ultimately plays itself out in behaviors throughout the organization—behaviors that are anything but polite, kind, or loving. When we get lost in our functional silos, we easily miss the answer to a critical question in any organization: What's everyone's job? To help the team win.

Ten tips for surviving corporate life

1. When you take a job in America, keep your eyes wide open. You are expendable. You can be fired at any time without cause. If you're in Europe, you have a hell of a lot more leverage after your initial trial period. In America, the company is king. Don't ever forget it.

2. There is a game to be played in corporate life. Figure out the rules, what's important, who the big dogs are, and what they want.

3. If you want to do well, crush your goals. Build strong relationships. Don't gossip and talk behind people's backs. Don't overshare things about your personal life. Anything can be used against you if and when the shit hits the fan.

4. Make your boss look good. That's half of your job. The other half is delivering on expectations.

5. You will be judged by how you look, what you say and do, and who you hang out with.

6. Make sure you have a life outside of work. I know too many workaholics who retired and have nothing, and I mean *nothing* to do. No hobbies, no interests. Guess what happens when they stop working full-time? They become miserable.

7. Do your best to understand the dynamics at the top of the house. Whatever goes on there influences everything else.

8. No organization is perfect. Accept what you can't change, and don't expect too much.

9. People aren't perfect. Just because someone has a big title doesn't mean they are enlightened. They're human and hopefully doing the best they can.

10. Take care of yourself and remember, you're a free agent. Keep the resumé up to date, know your worth in the market, and consistently build your network.
    Bonus tip: Set yourself apart by acting with the highest integrity no matter what the sharks are doing.

About the Author

Photo by Patricia Ramaer

Don Johnson is a former monk and business leader turned writer and executive coach. His spiritual quest began as a college student and led him on a ten-year journey where he lived in ashrams and taught meditation in North America, Europe, Africa and Australia.

In his thirties he left the ashram, started a family and a career in the leadership development industry where he provided training and coaching to leaders in Fortune 500 companies. He lives with his wife in a seacoast village in Scotland.

Get in touch with him at Don@bemoreconscious.com or visit his website at www.bemoreconscious.com